Dedication

*This book is dedicated to
my most precious resource,
my daughters Katherine and Laura*

Acknowledgments

Although they are anonymous, several families must be thanked for sharing information about their children for this book. Their information provided a reality base for the sample use of forms in Section III. Other families and colleagues must be thanked for their support and encouragement of this project. Specific individuals include Marci Wheeler, a social worker and friend from the Indiana Resource Center for Autism (IRCA); Cathy Pratt, the director of the IRCA and an advocate for families at the local and national level; and David Mank, executive director of the Indiana Institute on Disability and Community at Indiana University, where the IRCA is one of eight centers. Finally, the people of Autism Asperger Publishing Company must be thanked for their patience, support and belief in this project.

– B. A. V.

Table of Contents

Foreword

We began hiring one-to-one respite providers in 1988, when our son Jordan was 7 months old. He was a high-need baby, who had difficulty feeling comfortable with certain people and found it challenging to adjust to highly stimulating environments. Not knowing about his diagnosis of ASD until he was 2-1/2 years old made it difficult for us to put his unique needs into perspective. Besides, at that time, there was little information about ASD, and virtually no resources available to help one wisely hire and train a respite provider.

As a result, we embarked on our hiring journey with neither an instruction manual nor a road map. It was trial by fire, as we learned from our mistakes and gradually gained clarity about how to work effectively with providers. Eventually, I compiled all that we had learned into a book entitled *A "Stranger" Among Us: Hiring In-Home Support for a Child with ASD or other Neurological Differences* (2005), a guide to hiring and managing one-to-one providers.

This book takes up where "Stranger" leaves off. Beverly Vicker takes one crucial component of managing caregivers – sharing pertinent information – and provides a framework for clarifying and articulating all essential information regarding a child with ASD. Any provider working with a child whose family has taken advantage of this invaluable guide will be miles ahead in providing quality care for the individual child, as well as understanding key aspects of ASD, in general.

There are so many impressive features to this book. For example, in Section I, Beverly leaves no stone unturned in terms of outlining all the important information to compile about the child's needs and family routines, information that will help any provider feel more confident. An added benefit is that parents who take the time to fill out the worksheets will gain working knowledge about their family needs that will serve them in the long term in advocating effectively for their child.

I also love the philosophical foundation underlying the behavioral and communication strategies suggested in the book. Beverly clearly embraces the tenets of positive behavioral support. She skillfully departs from traditional behavioral management approaches that are so often ineffective in helping children with ASD understand what is expected of them.

This is an important book that fills a crucial gap in the literature. It is not only a helpful guide for families hiring paid respite providers, it should be part of any family's library to assist what Beverly refers to as "alternative caregivers" such as siblings, neighbors, extended family, and so on, in becoming proficient in providing care for a child with ASD. I am grateful that she has taken the time to compile and organize this crucial information into an invaluable resource for families.

– Lisa Ackerson Lieberman, MSW, LCSW

Introduction

Leaving one's child with an extended family member, neighbor, friend, paid respite, or an in-home care provider represents a potentially stressful situation for a parent who has a child with an an autism spectrum disorder (ASD). Parents may feel guilty about leaving the child, even though they need a break, need to spend quality time with a spouse or another son or daughter, or must take care of specific personal matters outside or inside the family home. Parents may be concerned about leaving their child for fear that someone else may not do things exactly the same way that they do, or they are worried that the caregiver won't understand the important issues relating to the child's special needs.

Despite such reservations, most parents end up using the services of an alternate care provider – whether paid or not – at some point. When that happens, the goal is to ensure the best possible care. Quality care begins with the careful selection of an alternate care provider. This process is extensively covered in an excellent book by Lisa Lieberman, *A "Stranger" Among Us: Hiring In-Home Support for a Child with Autism Spectrum Disorders or Other Neurological Differences* (2005). Whereas Lieberman's main focus is on the hiring process, the primary purpose of this resource is to help parents with the next step after selecting a caregiver – preparing someone for the job of caring for their loved one. Specifically, this book will help parents decide what information to share with these temporary or substitute caregivers to ensure that their child receives quality care during their absence regardless of whether the care is for a long or a short term.

While appropriate information sharing is imperative for the temporary, paid respite worker, some or all of the same information may be just as important for the unpaid respite worker (i.e., an extended family member, a neighbor, friend, older siblings), or the stepparent who may not have extensive experience providing care for the child with special needs. In addition, some of the information, with adaptation, may be equally important to share with more permanent childcare providers and teachers. Thus, although the term "respite worker" will be used throughout, its meaning is intended to include both professional and volunteer respite providers and others who need to know specific information about the child with ASD.

Brief Overview

The book is divided into five sections. Section I provides guidelines regarding the areas of child-specific information that parents may wish to share with other caregivers. This section is divided into two parts: basic information that will be somewhat stable over a period of time and a changeable section that is specific to the day(s) of care by the non-primary provider.

Section II provides background information in the form of generic topical information sheets to supplement the personal information and verbal instructions provided to the respite worker. An attempt has been made to keep the information on these pages short, easy-to-read and within the reading level of the typical respite worker (high school reading level). These topical handouts can be printed from the accompanying CD or copied directly from the book.

Section III contains examples of information for two different children. This section illustrates for readers how the preparation process might work.

Section IV contains blank forms that duplicate the format used in Section I. Parents may copy the forms and handwrite their notes. For parents who prefer to use a computer, we have included a CD with the pertinent forms. This allows parents to copy the master forms from the CD and then generate, store, and print the information via their home computer setup.

Finally, Section V contains references to optional material that a parent might wish to purchase or to suggest as reading/viewing material for caregivers who want more information. It also contains references that were consulted during the development and writing of this book.

While reading this book and completing the suggested forms may appear like a lot of extra work for the parent who is already challenged in terms of free time, careful preparation and subsequent updating of the information serves an important purpose: *providing the tools for respite workers to safely and reliably address your child's needs during your absence.* The payoff for parents will be that they have prepared a caregiver as best as they can and that they will be able to leave the home setting with greater peace of mind.

Section I – Deciding What to Share

- **Introduction/Overview**

- **I-A: Background Information**

- **I-B: Day-of-the-Event Information**

Getting Started – An Introduction and Overview of the Process

This section provides an orientation to the process of preparing for respite services and the support opportunities available in this book. The purpose of the book is to make both you and the respite worker or caregiver comfortable caring for your child. Topics covered include finding respite workers, deciding what information to share and using the blank pages or CD available via this book to provide background information, management information, and daily event information such as food for snacks, ideas for activities, and so forth. The questions in this section will help you think of important areas of information to consider sharing. Ultimately, you choose what you wish to share, but it helps to have some examples and guidance.

How Do I Find Good Respite Workers?

Information about respite resources specific to your geographic area is available from government or public agencies. For example, in Indiana, although the Indiana Resource Center for Autism (IRCA) retains a list of provider agencies on its website, the primary government contact is the Bureau of Developmental Disability – Case Management. The names of helpful agencies will vary by state. Your local library reference desk can guide you to appropriate resources if you are unable to access them yourself via a telephone book or a computer search. Other sources include teachers and friends who are familiar with respite services. The latter may be valuable in locating community respite agencies, but some of their advice and information may be insufficient or too general to guide you through the preparation process. Again, sources such as *A "Stranger" Among Us: Hiring In-Home Support for a Child with Autism Spectrum Disorders or Other Neurological Differences* (Lieberman, 2005) and others are great starting points.

In her book, Lieberman addresses such issues as questions to ask, warning signs about inappropriate candidates, importance of background checks, using employment contracts, guidelines about when and how to terminate a provider, and other important practical information. The book not only guides one through the procedural aspects of hiring help, but also enables parents to feel empowered as employers who are protective of their most precious resources – their children.

What Information Should I Share?

The bottom line is that what information you decide to share depends on who needs information and under what circumstances the information will be used. For example, you would probably leave different information for your child's grandmother if she sees him on a regular basis than for an infrequent paid stranger or your helpful-but-busy, multi-tasking next-door neighbor. Similarly, less information may be needed for the person who plays a supportive respite role while the whole family is vacationing. In contrast, extensive information would be generated for the sole person left behind to care for the child with special needs while the remainder of the family is on vacation.

If you use care providers for a variety of circumstances, you may consider preparing customized versions for each, or prepare a set for the person who is least familiar with the child and let everyone use the same materials, even if some of the material is not novel or unknown to them. This might save you time and confusion since there would only be one set of materials to keep updated.

The guiding directive for the entire endeavor of providing information for respite workers is to project yourself into the role of the respite worker. What would you want to know in order to feel comfortable and confident to handle routine situations as well as the unexpected ones that might occur in your household? Would you want some of the information in advance? Would you prefer personal instruction and demonstration from the parents and then depend upon the written information when you are alone and uncertain about what to do?

Put this perspective into a familiar medical analogy. You would likely feel more comfortable managing the medical care of an ill parent at home if you had information – both remembered and written – to guide you. Think how often people walk away from a doctor's office and only remember a fraction of what was said since supplementary print instruction was not provided. Remember the anxiety you felt when forgetting important information. By preparing ahead of time and sharing information, you can prevent your respite worker from feeling that way, and at the same time feel less anxious yourself knowing your child's needs will be met.

How Much Information Should I Share?

Each family has different needs and opinions regarding how much information to share with a respite worker concerning their child. For some children who are easy-going, have few sensory issues and limited behavioral challenges, minimal special information may be necessary for a short, at-home respite session. For others, with more severe needs, the parent may think that massive volumes are necessary. Different information may also be needed if the respite worker is taking the child into the community versus staying at home.

The challenge is to strike a balance – to share enough information about pertinent issues without going into such detail that the respite worker becomes overwhelmed. Not everything needs to be written down; sometimes an oral explanation or a demonstration is all that's needed. In addition, the respite worker may have past experiences that she can draw upon. It is essential, however, to have some written reference materials in order to reduce dependence on memory.

In general, it is probably better to err on the side of preparing too much than to assume that a given respite worker has all the necessary background knowledge. With this in mind, prepare the background information sheets in Section IV with guidance from Sections I and III and then select topic handout sheets from Section II that could give a deeper understanding of pertinent issues such as sensory challenges, suggested talking patterns, and positive programming. The handouts are short so each may easily be read within a few minutes. Don't view this as additional information to digest and remember. Instead, view it as a helpful illustration of information that you might discuss with the respite person.

Finally, an additional resource for answering the question of what information and how much to provide is found in the two case studies in Section III. Although there may appear to be some redundancy between the two cases, there are differences in the ages of the children, their special problems, the timing of the event, and the information left with the provider. The objective of each is to demonstrate what specific information might be shared and what might be the right amount of information to leave. It will be important to leave a guide to the information so a respite worker can quickly find what is needed without flipping through numerous pages.

When Should I Begin to Prepare the Information?

When possible, work through this book before you schedule respite services. Take time to think about what needs to be shared before putting together the written Background (I-A) material. Although Background Information (I-A) is prepared first, it probably will be placed after the Day-of-the-Event (I-B) material in the respite notebook. Consider having someone else review the Background (I-A) material to get feedback about clarity or possible oversights.

It is recommended that you have gathered all the necessary information when making that first contact with a prospective agency or individual. With a written set of information handy during a phone call or an interview, you are less likely to forget or overlook important information.

How Should I Prepare the Respite Worker for Caring for My Child?

Once you have prepared the Background (I-A) material and have a tentative list of supplementary handouts (Section II), you are ready for the first contact. The best way to prepare a new respite worker is to invite him to an advance visit to the family home. This allows you to share information in a more leisurely fashion, and at the same time, the child can become familiar with the provider and vice versa. During the initial visit, you may give the respite worker the child-specific background information (I-A) and generic topical sheets from Section III to read before returning for the scheduled respite event. You might even want to share some of the materials from the Day-of-the-Event (I-B) section if you have prepared them at this point. After reviewing the material ahead of time and thinking about the pending experience, the applicant is better able to formulate questions to ask on the first day of the scheduled event. During the visit, also show the person the first aid book, as suggested in Section V.

Some professional agencies do not automatically schedule an advance visit, though it is ideal. Sometimes finances, time, or circumstances make this practice prohibitive. If an advance visit is not possible, it might be better to pay the respite worker to shadow you and learn firsthand about how to manage your child in the course of a scheduled respite visit with you at home and in charge.

How Do I Use the Forms on the CD at the Back of the Book?

Put the CD into your CD drive and, once it has booted, open the program. Make a copy of each file if you plan to enter child-specific information; retain the master copy in its original state so you can copy it again, as needed. Enter text into the appropriate copy files. Update the Background Information (I-A) files discussed in the next section, as needed.

Generate new forms for the day of the event (I-B) for each respite event, or make several versions of some of the same sheets. Some of the same text may be copied to another file and modified for distribution to family members, teachers, and others. You can either print copies of the topic handouts from the master CD or download the files to your hard drive if you want to add comments. As you get familiar with Section II, you may find many uses for the handouts in addition to their use with the respite workers.

I-A: Background Information

This part includes many questions and suggestions for content to share about your child and your family. Some questions may seem trivial to you, but for other parents the questions may serve as an important reminder to share relevant information. The objective of the exhaustive lists is to make the task of generating selective information easier for parents. The topics occur in the following order:

- General family information
- General routines for family members
- Medical and disability information
- Self-help – eating, toileting, bathing, tooth brushing, dressing/ undressing and managing weather-related clothing, and getting to sleep
- Communication skills
- Play skills
- Sensory issues and fascinations
- Relaxation
- Transition
- Self-image
- Behavior (includes several subsections)

Use the suggestions as a guide in preparing the basic Background Information. Read through the entire section for a given subtopic such as "Self-Help – Eating." With a pencil, put a check mark by each area that is relevant to your child. Jot notes for yourself, as needed, or go directly to compose that page on the computer or on a paper copy. (See Section IV for blank forms or use the CD.) The blank forms do not repeat the questions. The forms are open-ended to encourage you to personally customize and summarize relevant information. This format allows you to combine information in a logical way that suits your style of writing.

Also, remember to check the case study examples in Section III. The examples were written for respite caregivers who had little previous experience with children with ASD and their special challenges. With the exception of the Behavior section, try to restrict information in any one subsection to 2-3 pages. Use an easy-to-read font and format; for example, consider using a 12- or 14-point font such as Times New Roman and double or 1-1/2 line spacing. Use red ink for emphasis of important information. Remember, you are not writing a novel, nor are you doing an assignment for an English class. Sentences do not have to be perfect. It is O.K. to use short sentences or even fragments such as bulleted phrases. Use whatever style feels comfortable. The important thing is to be explicit and clear.

Note: In the sections that follow, a child by the name of Jon will represent children with any type of autism spectrum disorder of either gender. It seemed more personable to use a child's name than to refer to "your child" or "your son or daughter" hundreds of times.

Topic Area: General Family Information

This section is intended to provide an introduction to your family. It probably will be read by the respite person before coming for the first visit and will serve as a refresher or reminder about your family for subsequent visits. This type of information is particularly important for someone who is new to your family or someone who is an infrequent caregiver for your child.

- List the members of the household and their names. Briefly share something about each family member.

- Provide the names and ages, where appropriate, of extended family members. Identify what each person is called by the family and what Jon calls each person. *Although a cousin may be named Melody, family members may call her "Sissy," and Jon may call her "Ity."*

- List Jon's legal name. (In case of an emergency, his medical charts would need to be located by his formal name.)

- List Jon's age and add a general comment so the provider does not make judgments based on body size or chronological age.

  Jon might be described as a happy 5-year-old, but in many ways he is more like a 2-year-old. He will need lots of supervision.

- Indicate if Jon wears a tracking device and if he is in the local first responders' (e.g., fire, police, and EMT departments) emergency database. Although this information also belongs on the Emergency sheet for the day of the event), be sure to include print information about this, or at least provide a verbal explanation of the services and the notation on the Emergency sheet.

- Add comments about the other children's interests, temperaments, and ability to help, if needed.

  Sara is 13 and very protective of Jon. She knows how to help calm him down.

- Provide the names and a description of all pets when the household contains more than one animal of the same species. Mention what each animal is called by the family versus what name Jon uses, if different.

- Identify other key people whom Jon may mention and identify the relationship.

  Some children just learning to talk may call their stepdad, birth father and all grandfathers by the title of "Dad." This can be confusing to a person unfamiliar with the family dynamics and the child's communication system. Even if the child uses a different name for different people, it might be important to know that Jon visits his birth dad every weekend, that Wendy is his stepmom, or that Jacob, whom Jon calls "Cub-Cub," is his favorite person at his preschool.

- Consider having a mini-photo album of key people if this would be helpful for clarity. (A photo book can also be a source for a joint attention activity with Jon.)

Topic Area: General Routines of Family Members

Knowing something about the typical routines of your family will prepare the respite worker for understanding the comings and goings and stressors upon your family. As Jon's difficulties with changes in routine are discussed in the transition section, the respite worker will have a global sense of how much family routine can be maintained in a specific household and the availability of each family member for backup support.

- List typical away-from-home and at-home schedules for each parent, at least in a general fashion.

  Dad is gone from 7 a.m. to 6 p.m. most weekdays; he is also out of town several days a month. On weekends and evenings, he often must be away from home to assist his ailing mother. Mom works part time in the mornings while Jon is in school. In her free time, she is always busy providing transportation for the other two children since the family lives in the country and the children are too young to drive.

- List Jon's typical daily routine.

  Jon attends preschool five mornings a week. In the afternoons, he has occupational therapy and speech therapy twice a week and music therapy once a week. He likes to take a nap, if possible, in the afternoon. His weekends consist of free time and accompanying the family on outings.

- List the routine of siblings.

Sara leaves at 6:45 in the morning for school, and some days she doesn't come home until 6 p.m. She is active in gymnastics and after-school lessons and has meets on Saturday. Some days she studies with friends at their homes after school; frequently several friends come over to the house after school or on the weekend. Bryan often spends hours on the computer when he comes home. Sometimes he rides his bike down the road to a classmate's home.

- List any rules that apply for Jon and for his siblings when the parents are not home.

The rules may be that when a respite worker is in the house, the siblings cannot have friends come over, or that neither of the children in the example above (Sara and Bryan) is allowed to leave the house to be with friends. Further, Jon may not watch – regardless of what arguments he raises – certain videos because they cause him to have nightmares, and he may not watch any reality-TV shows where people do outrageous stunts.

Topic Area: Medical and Disability Information

This section presents some crucial capsulated information about Jon. In a direct fashion, it can say to the caregiver, "You need to be sure you know how to manage medications, be alert for certain side effects, understand the challenges, and know how to adapt your behavior to make this experience a positive one for our child and for you. Be sure you ask questions so you really understand what you are facing."

- List the disabilities that are relevant to Jon's care and well-being. For example, it would be important to identify Jon as having an autism spectrum disorder. Sharing information about some cognitive difficulties, hearing or vision problems, seizure disorder, Tourette's, attention deficit disorder, or other difficulties would be helpful.

- List whether Jon is on any medications; advise about side effects, if necessary.

- Indicate whether it is likely that any medications will need to be administered during a respite visit. It is not necessary to list them on this sheet. Instead, put them on the forms for Day-of-the-Event information. List where the medications are kept and how they are secured. If administration is needed, what procedures are used? Also put this information into the Day-of-the-Event section on Medication.

Even if it is unlikely that medications will need to be administered on a given day, it might be a good idea for the caregiver to know where the medications are and how to administer them in case of an emergency. No one pre-plans events like car accidents or traffic jams, but when an unforeseen delay occurs and your child needs medication on a certain time schedule, it is better that the caregiver knows what to do following your emergency phone call.

- List whether Jon has any allergies, and if so, to what. This information might be repeated in the Day-of-the-Event section. By putting it in both the advance information section (Background Information) and the current event section (Day-of-the-Event), you are increasing the likelihood that the respite worker will be aware of and will remember this crucial information.

- List whether Jon has other frequent health issues such as ear infections, stomachaches, headaches, and so forth.

- List whether Jon's pain threshold is different from most other children. Explain the implications of this common characteristic for many children with ASD.

- List whether Jon is reliable in perceiving and communicating pain. For example, if he indicates that his head hurts, is it usually his head and not a more distant site such as his stomach? Can he point to a body part or does he need to use a visual chart?

- List what behaviors or signs might suggest that Jon is not feeling well.

- List any dangerous behaviors that Jon engages in that could result in him (or others) getting hurt. List this in bold print and underline in red.

- List anything else not covered elsewhere that relates to safety and emergency situations.

Topic Area: Self-Help

*There are numerous situations where trust is needed in the area of self-help. Parents are often concerned about abuse of their children. At the same time, respite workers and other caregivers may be reluctant to engage in care that could be perceived as questionable. This is particularly true in the areas of toileting, dressing and undressing, bathing, and bedtime routines, especially with children who need extensive physical assistance. Some teachers report that they try to avoid physically touching **any** child; this represents an extreme self-protective response as a consequence of abuse accusations reported in the media.*

Following up on the references of the respite worker and interviewing the person before a respite event can help alleviate concerns for your child's safety. Lieberman's book (2005) referenced earlier includes helpful information regarding screening prospects and the interview process. Some risk taking will always be necessary, but if parents want total peace of mind, they may wish to consider the use of miniature video cameras in key areas of the house.

Once you have taken whatever measures you think are necessary in this area, be sure to be clear about what is needed and why, so that both parents and the worker can feel comfortable about the support needed and the appropriate boundaries.

Topic: Self-Help – Eating

Mealtimes or the task of eating can be stressful for many children. Give as much information as needed to ensure successful meal and snack time events.

☐ Does Jon use/need any visual sequence charts, food portion allowance charts or other visual display to help him with mealtime routines?

☐ Can Jon eat independently or does he need assistance? If he needs assistance, does this only apply to select foods or to all food substances?

☐ Does Jon use a spoon, knife, and fork, or does he only eat finger foods?

☐ Are special cups or plates needed as part of Jon's mealtime routine? If so, where are they kept? What do they look like?

☐ Do any foods need to be cut up for Jon?

☐ Does Jon stuff his face with food if given the whole portion at once? Should he only be given small amounts at a time? If so, how small is "small"? Does he only get one food at a time on his plate or does he get various foods?

☐ Does Jon have difficulty swallowing? Does he easily choke? Is he likely to spit out food, and if so, how is this handled? (You can mention strategies in the Behavior section if this happens often.)

☐ What are Jon's favorite foods, most disliked foods, and foods that need to be avoided because of allergies? (The latter is also recorded in the Day-of-the-Event information.)

☐ Does Jon engage in pica, or the eating of inedible items? Are there some inedible items that he puts in his mouth but doesn't swallow? If yes, what does he swallow or hold in his mouth? Indicate how to safely remove the object from his mouth before he swallows it. (This may also be discussed in the Behavior section.)

☐ Does Jon throw food? If yes, how is this to be handled? (You can mention this and discuss strategies in the Behavior section.)

☐ What strategies should be used if Jon refuses to eat at a regular mealtime?

☐ Does Jon usually eat at scheduled mealtimes and snack times or is he allowed to eat anytime he wants?

☐ Does Jon sit at the family table, a child-size table, or in a high-chair? How long will he sit to eat? Does he graze from finger food bowls on a random basis instead of sitting at the table? Are any special adaptations or allowances made for him at mealtime?

☐ Does Jon use a bib? If so, is it a specific one? How does he react if his shirt or hands get dirty? Is there a trick to helping him have a clean face when the meal is over? Can Jon wipe his own mouth, if reminded, or does he need help? If he needs help, how does he react to someone trying to wipe it for him? What is used for wiping his face?

☐ How do you know if Jon is hungry outside of scheduled meal or snack times?

☐ What are favorite stand-by foods in case Jon doesn't want what is on the Food for the Day chart (if this is an acceptable practice by your standards)?

☐ Is Jon expected to take his dishes to the sink or counter when he is finished?

☐ Any other important information relative to eating?

Topic Area: Self-Help – Toileting

Toileting can be a challenge for a child with ASD. Be sure your substitute care provider understands what helps or hinders your child from successfully managing or coping with toileting situations. Many steps are involved in the toileting or changing process. Maintaining the usual routine may spell the difference between keeping your child in a comfort zone or raising his anxiety level. Details are important.

☐ Is Jon independent in managing his toileting needs (i.e., he recognizes a need to go and can manage all the tasks involved without assistance)?

☐ Does Jon ask permission to go to the bathroom or announce that this is what he is going to do?

☐ Does Jon use a picture- or text-based sequence display to guide him through the routine?

☐ Does Jon reliably recognize body signals for both urination and bowel movement, or does he still have accidents in one or both areas?

☐ Does Jon routinely get up during the night to go to the bathroom? If so, does he need assistance in order to go back to bed or to use the bathroom? How often does he wake up to go to the bathroom after falling asleep? Is there a particular time that he tends to awaken?

☐ How often does Jon typically go to the bathroom during the day?

☐ Does he tell someone when he needs assistance and what type of help he needs?

☐ Does Jon need help with fastening and unfastening clothing?

☐ Does Jon experience pain during bowel movements? If so, explain what the respite worker is to do or say to help the situation.

☐ Does he need help with wiping himself or with washing and drying his hands?

☐ Does Jon need help flushing the toilet when he is finished?

☐ If Jon is not independent, what toileting routine do you use?

☐ Is Jon on a time-determined toileting schedule? If so, what is the time interval?

☐ If he is not on a schedule, how does one know when he needs to use the bathroom? Does he verbally indicate a need? Use gestures? Or, does the care provider have to note when he might be grabbing his crotch or some other nonverbal sign?

☐ What is the routine for toileting? Does he stand or sit to urinate? When he sits, does he use a potty chair or the regular toilet? If the latter, is a special seat used?

☐ Are there cue words or phrases associated with the routine?

☐ Does Jon want someone to stay in the bathroom with him while he is toileting?

☐ How long does he generally need to sit for a bowel movement?

☐ What is the procedure if Jon still wears diapers or pull-ups? Where does changing normally take place? Where are the spare diapers and wipes located?

☐ Will spare clothing be left out in case Jon has an accident and needs to change clothes?

☐ Does Jon stay dry when he is asleep? If not, does he wear special diapers? Where are the diapers kept?

☐ How cooperative is Jon for the changing routine? If not cooperative, how does one successfully manage the situation?

☐ What is the routine for dealing with wet clothing and/or sheets if he urinates while asleep?

☐ What is the procedure for disposing of a diaper?

☐ Where are the protective gloves kept to perform changing or dealing with the clean-up of body fluids?

☐ Are there other specific problems that relate to elimination needs (e.g., smearing feces)? How can these be managed or avoided?

☐ Any other important information relative to toileting?

Topic Area: Self-Help – Bathing

Bath time can be fraught with sensory and behavioral challenges. To refresh your memory, record what happens over several bath time events so you can character-ize the essence of what needs to happen, could happen, or should not happen. If your child does not take a bath every night, you might want the respite worker to skip bath time. Neverthe-less, complete this section in case a bath needs to occur.

If the respite worker will be taking your child into the community, specifically if the activity involves swimming and a required shower, write out a separate set of all the steps, especially if your child is in-flexible and likely to create a scene if the familiar does not occur.

☐ Does John bathe or shower independently? Can he turn on the water and regulate the temperature and flow? Can he wash all body parts, shampoo when necessary, dry off, and get into other clothes? If not in total, what parts can he do independently?

☐ Are there points during the bathing routine when he needs supervision or assistance? If so, which ones?

☐ How long does the shower or bath last? Will Jon terminate on his own or need a reminder of the limit? If he needs a reminder, how is it communicated? What happens if he re-fuses to honor that limit?

☐ Can he get his own things ready for the shower or bath?

☐ Does he need to shampoo or be shampooed in the bathtub, shower or sink?

☐ Does he need reminders to wash specific body parts or to use soap? Are there certain body parts that he always skips, if not reminded?

☐ What is the routine for a bath or shower? Does bathing take place at a certain time or at a certain juncture of the schedule? What is the order of events prior to, during, and after the bath or shower?

☐ Are specific toys, soaps, or towels part of the routine?

☐ Are specific words or phrases part of the routine?

☐ Does he use a visual schedule to help him get through the routine?

☐ Is a sibling likely to want to take a bath with Jon, and is this permitted?

☐ Do specific behaviors sometimes occur during the bathing scenario such as dumping water on the floor? What are these behaviors? How can they be avoided? How should the caregiver handle the scenario if it does happen?

☐ Any other important information relative to bathing?

Topic Area: Self-Help – Tooth Brushing

Tooth brushing is a necessary daily routine that involves a specific sequence and potential sensory challenges for a child with ASD. Observe your child's routine and note the adaptations that may be important to share.

☐ When, where, and how often does Jon brush his teeth each day? Are the times tied to clock time or to events, such as after meals?

☐ Does Jon use a visual sequence chart (objects, pictures, or text) to guide the tooth brushing process?

☐ Can Jon go and brush his teeth if told to do so, or will he need assistance and/or supervision?

☐ If Jon is independent, what is the routine?

☐ If Jon needs supervision, what is the routine? What aspects of the routine need supervision? What happens if he attempts to skip part of the routine or does a superficial job (i.e., is he given a verbal reminder, physical assistance, modeling, etc.)?

☐ If Jon is semi-independent or dependent, what is the routine? Do you do anything special or have him do anything unique to mark time or duration for the brushing? For example, he might brush while you sing a song or until you reach a certain number while counting.

☐ How cooperative is Jon in terms of performing/tolerating the routine? What helps him be more cooperative? If he chooses to not be cooperative, what needs to be done?

☐ What social or tangible reward is given if tooth brushing is accomplished according to your expectations? If Jon is praised, does he expect certain phrases to be said? Do you engage in a nonverbal ritual such as a high five? If a sticker or some other tangible object is used, where are the reinforcers kept, and what is the routine for delivering them?

☐ Any other important information relative to tooth brushing?

Topic Area: Self-Help – Dressing/Undressing/ Managing Weather-Related Clothing

This section includes three different types of tasks. Undressing and dressing are motor skills with undressing mastered before dressing. Unless you specifically let the caregiver know what you expect your child to do, your child may be passive and get unneeded assistance. Conversely, because you are not the one helping, the child may attempt to do things independently, even if he or she does not yet have the skills, in order to avoid performing the familiar activity with a stranger.

Managing weather-related clothing involves other skills and considerations such as cognition, flexibility, and sensory challenges. Some children do not have the ability to make good judgments about what type of clothing is needed relative to specific weather conditions. Others may be able to follow a rule but are not reflective to consider that they may prefer to be cooler than most people in warm weather. Issues related to managing weather-related clothing also include coping with the transition from heavy clothing to lighter clothing, and vice versa, as the weather/temperature changes.

Undressing

☐ Can Jon comply with requests to get totally *undressed* at the appropriate time, or does he need supervision and/or assistance? Is there a difference between his ability to handle indoor/outdoor weather-related clothing and wet swim trunks? Be sure to discuss the different types of clothing situations, if necessary.

☐ What type of direct assistance is needed? Is the respite worker supposed to wait to be asked, or does he ask Jon if he needs assistance? At which points in the routine should assistance be automatically given?

☐ How far away and where does the adult usually position herself, if distance is an important consideration? What are the difficult steps and what cues or directions are offered?

☐ Does Jon, on his own initiative, undress totally or partially at inappropriate times? If so, how is this handled?

Dressing

☐ Can Jon be told to get dressed and then do it by himself? Is there a difference between his ability to manage indoor versus outdoor weather-related clothing? Be sure to discuss both dressing conditions.

☐ Will Jon need to make any decisions about what he needs to put on, or will a set of clothes already be selected?

☐ Is Jon reluctant to wear or put on any particular piece or type of clothing? If he refuses, is this acceptable during the respite worker's stay? For example, Jon may like to run around barefoot and without a shirt, regardless of the temperature indoors or outdoors.

☐ How should the respite worker handle any protests about what Jon is to wear, if refusal is not an option?

☐ What type of supervision is needed when Jon gets himself dressed? Will he ask for help or respond to the inquiry of whether or not he needs help?

☐ What types of clothing are difficult for Jon to manage on his own?

☐ How should help be provided? If Jon needs total or partial assistance, identify the routine and how help is provided.

☐ Is Jon sensitive to any body part being touched or covered? For example, Jon may not like his head to be touched or his vision blocked when a pullover shirt goes over his head.

☐ If Jon is resistant to assistance, what strategies do you suggest?

☐ Is there anything else that should be shared about your child and clothing, even if it doesn't directly relate to dressing/undressing? For example, even though this might be also stated in the Sensory section, it might be helpful to share that Jon likes to wear long-sleeved shirts regardless of the weather. This will help the respite worker select a replacement in case Jon dirties his clothes and needs to change.

☐ Any other important information relative to dressing/undressing and weather-related clothing?

Topic Area: Self-Help – Getting to Sleep

Getting children ready for bed and to sleep is a trial for many parents, not just parents of children with special needs. Children who are otherwise relatively easy to manage in the daytime may be less flexible and adaptable when irritated and tired. Conveying the essence of the bedtime routine for others is imperative if you hope to arrive home after an evening activity to find your child fast asleep.

☐ Does Jon need to engage in quieter activities as bedtime approaches? How far in advance and what types of activities are off limits once a certain time is a reached? For example, chase games, wrestling, video games, and suspense-filled movies may elevate the sensory system rather than facilitate calming and relaxation.

☐ What is the typical bedtime routine? Is a picture or text schedule part of the routine?

☐ Is book reading a part of the routine? If so, provide enough information so the respite worker knows which books to read and for how long.

☐ Does Jon want any specific adaptations to help him sleep, such as rolling him into a quilt, zipping him into a sleeping bag, allowing him to sleep on the floor with or in his sleeping bag, or turning on a fan as a masking noise?

☐ Do you routinely do anything else to assist Jon in getting to sleep (e.g., massage, music, a specific level of lighting, the presence of an adult in the room in a chair, sitting by the bed, or an adult lying near him on the bed)?

☐ What should the caregiver do if Jon is resistant to settling down or staying in bed? Is he allowed to drink or eat anything once in bed? Are additional trips to the bathroom necessary or merely part of stalling?

☐ Are siblings allowed to sleep with Jon in his room? Conversely, is it O.K. for Jon to sleep with his siblings in their rooms?

☐ Does Jon have any nighttime fears about thunder, lightning, or other things? How are these fears managed?

☐ Does Jon have night terrors (e.g., screaming while still in a sleep state)?

☐ How long does it typically take for him to fall asleep?

☐ How likely is Jon to stay asleep through the night? What is the routine if he awakens?

☐ If Jon falls asleep somewhere other than his bed before bedtime, what should be done?

☐ If Jon takes a nap, what is the routine? How long does he typically sleep?

☐ Does Jon take a bottle, pacifier, or special blanket to bed with him? Where are the special items kept?

☐ Any other important information relative to sleeping?

Topic Area: Communication Skills

It is essential that the respite worker understands Jon's comprehension level and his ability to communicate under optimal conditions as well as while he is stressed, overly stimulated, or anxious. The respite worker may need special training in this area in addition to written information. He needs to be aware of Jon's difficulties reading the verbal and nonverbal messages of others. He will also need to be familiar with the special meaning of some of Jon's nonverbal and verbal behaviors if they are different from what most people might interpret. For example, it is easy to overestimate a child's level of understanding if she uses echolalia that sounds too sophisticated for her age.

☐ Does Jon primarily use verbal speech to communicate? How proficient is he at generating new messages that fit a situation?

☐ How well do strangers or unfamiliar people understand Jon's speech?

☐ Do you have any suggestions to assist in understanding Jon's speech? For example, it might be helpful to know that Jon is very literal in his speech as well as in his understanding of the speech of others.

☐ Does Jon get angry and verbally abusive to anyone? Please provide strategies or discuss in the Behavior section. Is he likely to appear angry because you have left him behind with a stranger?

☐ Does he swear? If so, how is this handled? (Some respite workers might be shocked if not warned ahead of time.)

☐ Can the respite worker depend on Jon to use his verbal communication skills to let her know his needs and concerns?

☐ Does Jon talk excessively? If so, what is the best way to deal with it?

☐ What topics represent his obsessions? Are there other topics he enjoys talking about that are not obsessive?

☐ Does he ask a lot of questions of others? Would any of them be perceived as too personal? (It is better to let the respite worker know what to expect, if possible.)

☐ Is Jon echolalic and, if so, how much of what he says is repetition of what he has heard others say?

☐ Are there echolalic phrases that Jon uses that have particular meaning that a stranger is not likely to figure out? (Consider providing an advance interpretation for frequent, important "messages.")

☐ If Jon is nonverbal or minimally verbal (i.e., only has a few functional words), how does he communicate deliberately? Does Jon use gestures, sign language, picture exchange, communication display, or an augmentative communication device? Explain in person how to use these adaptations and consider using a supplementary handout from Section II. Prepare a picture list of key signs used. Be sure the respite person knows where the communication board, picture cards, or device are/is kept.

☐ How does Jon use these augmentative communication methods? How does a respite worker encourage him to use these means of communication or understand his system? Use demonstration to clarify the situation, when possible.

☐ Does Jon always communicate deliberately? Does the adult frequently have to figure out his messages or "read the situation" when he is not deliberately communicating his thoughts, needs, or concerns? Can the respite worker easily guess from environmental clues the probable meaning of the messages?

☐ How would you describe Jon's social communication/interaction behavior?

☐ Does Jon give eye contact when he is communicating with someone?

☐ Does he have difficulty keeping an appropriate distance from his communication partner, or does he stand too close?

☐ Does he engage in inappropriate touching of others when communicating with them and, if so, how is this handled? (This may be covered under the Sensory section instead.)

☐ Does Jon take turns when having a conversion or is communication limited to one turn on a topic?

☐ Does Jon initiate, or does he primarily respond to initiations by others?

☐ Does Jon respond positively or negatively to a speaker who is very animated and bubbly?

☐ Is Jon more responsive to a loud, average or soft tone/volume of voice?

☐ If Jon tires of someone's attempt to interact or be with him, what does he do? How does he signal that he needs some quiet, more space, or fewer demands?

☐ How would you describe Jon's ability to comprehend the verbal speech of others?

☐ Does Jon understand better if a person speaks at a slower than normal rate? Does he do better with short sentences, such as 3-5 words per sentence?

☐ Does Jon have difficulty with directions? How do you phrase specific directions, and is there anything special about how you give the directions? For example, do you use visual supports such as pictures or gestures?

☐ Does Jon have difficulty understanding questions?

☐ Should the respite worker monitor her vocabulary to aid Jon in comprehending her communication to him? Describe what happens when Jon does not understand. For example, does he walk away or stand and do nothing?

☐ Are there special words that need to be used? For example, his pacifier may only be recognized by the term "binkie."

☐ Does Jon like someone to read to him? Does he have favorite books? Do you read the text or just talk about the pictures? Does he need to look at the book first before he will look at it with someone else?

☐ Any other important information relative to communication?

Topic Area: Play Skills

Play or free time may occupy much of the time of a respite visit. Some children with ASD who are good at occupying themselves with their special interests may be less interested in interactive play with the care provider. Others may have very little ability to occupy themselves and need considerable structure and adult support. Be sure the caregiver understands your child and how to best meet his needs during what could be long hours of childcare.

☐ How does Jon amuse himself during free time or downtime?

☐ Does Jon need someone to entice him into play activities? If so, how is this best achieved?

☐ What is Jon's attention span when playing with his favorite toys?

☐ Does he tolerate and/or enjoy someone playing parallel to him (i.e., someone is nearby but playing independently)?

☐ Does he tolerate and/or enjoy someone interacting with him during play?

☐ Does Jon have preconceived ideas of what the adult should do during a play routine, and will he get upset if someone doesn't know the routine? Or, is he somewhat flexible and interested in novelty?

☐ Is wandering or pacing a cue that some structured play or work activity should be offered to Jon?

☐ Are Jon's siblings good playmates for him? What supervision or suggestions from an adult might be necessary to help the play activity be successful? Is it better for Jon to play alone or with the respite provider?

☐ Is it O.K. for Jon to engage in repetitive play, such as lining up cars, if he is happy doing it? Sometimes this is a good option when the child doesn't know the caregiver.

☐ Are there safety issues to be concerned about during indoor play?

☐ What should be expected if Jon is taken outside to play? What are his typical behaviors and routines? Are there safety concerns with outdoor play? For example, is he likely to climb a fence, bolt for the street, hide in a secret place, or attempt to entice the adult to chase him by running away?

☐ What indoor and outdoor activities are absolutely forbidden?

☐ Are there any activities that might be off limits for most children but that you allow Jon to do?

☐ What is his level of interest in books? What are the routines associated with looking at various types of books? For example, some children touch pictures and want the adult to name the object. (You may have described this adequately in the Communication section but may wish to repeat here.)

☐ What type of indoor play most attracts his interest? For example, motor activities such as climbing or being chased, manipulative tasks like puzzles, sorting objects, or looking at books. What attracts him most when he is outdoors?

☐ Is Jon allowed to operate the TV, computer, VCR, DVD player, or stereo without adult assistance? What are the rules for use, content, length of time, and so forth? (This information may be included on the Activities sheet in the Day-of-the-Event section, but it is helpful to list here as well.)

☐ What types of activities do you think would be most suitable during your absence? (You may want to jot down some ideas and select from this list when you design the Activities sheet for the Day-of-the-Event.)

☐ If Jon is a runner, how is he prevented from going outside on his own? What is the alarm/lock system on the doors? Does he wear a tracking device? (Describe here or in the Behavior section.)

☐ Any other important information relative to play behavior?

Topic Area: Sensory Issues and Fascinations

An understanding of sensory issues strikes at the heart of support for a child with ASD. Each child has individual challenges, so it is important to delineate your child's situation. What may have worked for a previous child seen by the respite worker may be totally wrong for yours. Be sure the caregiver is aware of your child's unique needs, and review all the sensory areas that are relevant for your child.

☐ Is Jon sound sensitive? What immediate sounds are most bothersome to him? What does he do when he is uncomfortable? What might an adult do to help him?

☐ Does Jon seek out any particular type of auditory stimulation, including music?

☐ Are there certain types of situations that Jon tries to avoid because he doesn't like the noise associated with it? (Some children try to avoid a public restroom because of the loud noise of the commodes when flushing.)

☐ Does Jon have more difficulty listening to instruction or concentrating if there is significant background noise?

☐ Does Jon go into sensory overload if exposed to lots of sound over a period of time?

☐ Does Jon have any atypical responses or preferences regarding temperature? For example, does he need to use cold water to wash his hands?

☐ Can Jon be trusted to turn on a water faucet and achieve a water temperature that would not be too hot for his skin?

☐ Do food or beverages need to be at a certain temperature for Jon to consume them?

☐ Does Jon monitor the temperature of food, or does the adult need to caution him that something may be too hot?

☐ Does Jon like to feel warm or cool in terms of clothing regardless of the temperature of the immediate environment? (Explain rather than give a one-word response unless covered well in the Dressing section.)

☐ Is Jon sensitive to textures, such as food, clothing, or objects such as a hair brush? (Explain the sensitivity and how it is managed.)

☐ Does Jon have issues with being touched by anyone when not initiated by him? What types of touch elicit negative reactions?

☐ Does Jon have special spatial boundaries that need to be recognized and respected? For example, Jon doesn't like peers to come within three feet of the structures he builds with blocks.

☐ Does Jon seek out any type of touch or physical pressure? Describe what type of touch he seeks (light or deep) and how he seeks it. How should the respite worker respond? Does he always like a particular type of touch, or does it vary? If the latter, how will the respite worker know which touch is needed in a given situation?

☐ Is Jon compulsively drawn to touch certain types of objects or body parts, such as someone's hair? What attracts his attention, and how is this best managed? (The strategies may be described in the Behavior section.)

☐ What particular foods or objects does Jon prefer to eat or lick? What types of foods does he dislike from the perspective of taste – salty, sour, bland, sweet?

☐ Is Jon sensitive to certain types of smells or odors? What does he dislike, and what attracts him?

☐ Is Jon attracted to particular types of visual stimuli? What general types of visual stimuli capture his attention; for example, movement such as fluttering or spinning, patterns specific colors, or shapes? Conversely, are there any shapes, patterns, or colors, that he intensely dislikes? For example, a child who does not like blue may dislike a person if she has blue eyes.

☐ Is TV/DVD/video viewing one of Jon's fixations? What happens when he watches? Are there particular programs/games that he likes? How much is he allowed to watch? How is he to be distracted from watching or wanting to watch?

☐ Is Jon addicted to using the computer for visual stimulation? How is this managed?

☐ Is text (i.e., printed words, the alphabet, or numbers) a fixation for Jon?

☐ Does Jon finger flick? Is this a preoccupation or a sign of agitation?

☐ If Jon escalates in terms of excitement because of visual stimulation, how is this managed?

☐ Does Jon use any movements, such as rocking or pacing, to help himself deal with stress or anxiety?

☐ Is Jon well or poorly coordinated for his age in terms of fine- and gross-motor skills?

☐ Does Jon need access to particular sensory activities in order to be happy or calm? If so, what are they? Is there a time limit for engaging in these activities? What should the caregiver do if his excitement level escalates?

☐ How is masturbation or the touching by Jon of his private parts viewed by the family? How are these behaviors managed? Be sure the caregiver is able to respond consistently with the family's wishes versus her personal beliefs.

☐ Does Jon have any unusual obsessions or interests, such as an obsession with shoes or lint?

☐ Do any of Jon's interests present a safety concern? How is this obsession handled in a safe manner?

☐ Any other important information relative to sensory issues?

Topic Area – Relaxation

Every person usually responds to some taught or self-devised techniques that reduce stress, including listening to relaxation tapes, exercising, drinking a beverage, watching a favorite video, or looking at magazines. It is imperative that the respite worker knows how to help your child relax. You know what works – you use Strategy X if he is mildly agitated and Strategy Z if he is bouncing off the walls. Make sure your information in this area will guide the substitute caregiver to the appropriate strategy and support for a variety of circumstances.

☐ How will the respite worker know that Jon is getting anxious or overstimulated and that he needs to relax?

☐ Does Jon recognize when he is overstimulated or anxious and needs to relax? What does he do, on his own, to try to help himself feel better?

☐ Can Jon be told to relax or engage in a specific relaxation routine and will he independently follow through with the routine? Are specific words or visual supports used to identify the stress level, such as "You are a four on the chart. You need to relax. Let's go find the rocking chair."?

☐ If the adult needs to direct the relaxation efforts, should a choice of techniques be offered? What are the techniques that Jon knows? Are they on a menu or choice card? How much cuing and support is needed to help him relax?

☐ How will the respite worker know if Jon has engaged in the relaxation activity long enough?

☐ Should the caretaker be concerned if Jon seems to engage in the relaxation activity for a long time? What would be considered excessive, and how does one intervene to stop?

☐ How does the caregiver get Jon to move on to another activity, or will he automatically know when he feels ready to do something else?

☐ Any other important information relative to relaxation?

Topic Area – Transition

Transitions represent time and space junctures that can cause anxiety and major behavior problems for the child with ASD. Sometimes the difficulty reflects a lack of information about what is going to happen; sometimes it reflects a challenge in stopping an activity that may be incomplete and shifting to another; sometimes it includes avoidance of the place or task to which the child is supposed to transition. Because transitions can be volatile or anxiety producing, it is important to share information about how to make transitions happen smoothly and easily in whatever environments respite services will occur.

- How does Jon manage transitions:

    o From place to place (familiar or new)?

    o From activity to activity?

    o From step to step within an activity?

    o From person to person?

- What seems to be the underlying challenge for transitions? Does he have a hard time stopping something unless there is a clearly marked ending?

- Does Jon perseverate on given steps and have difficulty stopping or moving on? Does he have some characteristics of movement difference, such as perseverative movement and the appearance of being unable to stop a movement and shift out of an activity on his own?

- Does Jon have a strong need to control everything so that rejection of a requested transition is a manifestation of that need?

- Does Jon avoid transitions because he has a strong need to complete a task? Is he aware that some tasks have sequential steps and that he may return to the task at a later time?

- What is Jon's understanding of time? Does he understand what is meant by a 5-minute warning? How aware is he of the passage of time? Can he estimate how long it will take to do something to completion? Does he know when 5 minutes have passed? Do you use a timer to help?

- Is he fearful about moving to a different situation because he needs more information about what will happen there?

- What strategies do you use to help Jon effectively manage various types of transitions? (Some of this might also be discussed in the Behavior section if transition issues are viewed as a major behavior problem.)

- Any other important information relative to transitions?

Topic Area – Self-Image

We all have a self-image. It is important that the respite worker understand the parameters of self-image as it pertains to your child and his perspective. Self-image is sometimes at the basis of behavioral issues, especially for some very verbal students. Many of these children have a sense that they must be perfect; for example, they must know all the answers and never make a mistake.

☐ Does Jon have specific issues relating to his self-image? Is he concerned that others must see him as intelligent? Can he accept making a mistake?

☐ Must Jon win every competition or game?

☐ Does Jon have unusual internal rules that he expects others to follow? Do you always know what the rules are?

☐ Does he like being seen as a helper?

☐ Is he often depressed and/or anxious? Is there a concern that he is suicidal?

☐ Any other important information to share relative to self-image?

Topic Area – Behavior

Behavioral issues have been placed last in this discussion of relevant topics, only because this topic requires a different format for the preparation of information than the other topics. In terms of importance, it might be placed at or near the front of the notebook for both the Day-of-the-Event and Background Information sections.

You want the respite worker and your child to have a successful experience with each other. You also want to hire good respite workers who are interested in returning to your household to provide care. Therefore, it is important to adequately prepare your respite worker for managing behaviors. Remember, you are putting information into written format so the person can easily refer to the printed information as challenges arise and/or, if in a heightened state of anxiety, she has forgotten your message about behavior management. Remember to keep the directions/information to a manageable level; do not write volumes of notes that will be difficult to read, process, and integrate.

Examples appear after the directions for this section and in the two case studies in Section III. The examples in the book may be more detailed than what you need or feel comfortable preparing. The examples are just that – examples, and not a requirement that your worksheets must look just like them. Any amount of information for reference will be appreciated by your respite worker. Dealing with the Behavior section can take work the first time, so don't avoid this section until the last minute.

Worksheet A – The Guiding Outline

Worksheet A is not an outline per se such as you may associate with writing a term paper in high school or college. Instead, it provides a quick overview of the total picture regarding behavior. Worksheet A can accommodate two different uses. First, it provides you with a rough draft of items to discuss on the subsequent worksheets; for example, what one will see, why your child may be doing the behavior and what to do to manage the behavior. Second, that working list can be formalized on another copy of Worksheet A as a quick guide for the respite worker.

On Worksheet A, in the rough draft version, list what your immediate family views as problem behaviors in the first column. Then, add what others consider as problem behaviors that are not mentioned on your list. The latter may include problems noted by extended family members, teachers, and so forth. Remember, behavior problems are often in the eye of the beholder. What you have learned to ignore or consider minor may be considered a problem by someone else. Review the list of behaviors. Cross off the ones that are VERY unlikely to happen at home during the respite stay. These may include problems specific to being in particular situations in the community or situations that you know will not happen at home during your absence. For example, if shampooing is a traumatic experience for your child, you may not even ask a respite worker to perform that duty. If you guess wrong, the caregiver may need to call you, or she will do the best she can given other information you have left for her. You can amend the list for the next visit.

All you can do is prepare the worker as best as you can and recognize that it may not be 100% perfect. Later, you will describe each behavior in more detail on Worksheet B-1. By describing it in more detail, you can be sure you and the respite worker are talking about the same thing. Otherwise, there will be confusion or inconsistency of responses to your child. For example, if you say "hitting" is a behavior, your respite worker could be looking for a hard, angry hit, and you may be discouraging even a light hit with a redirect to a relaxation chair.

In the second column, list what you think might be the purpose(s) of the behavior. You may need to guess and there may be multiple reasons for some behaviors that vary by circumstance. Because you are making this out ahead of time, if you don't have a clue about why, take time to observe the behavior and then step back and think about what might have been behind the behavior and what you have found to be effective for managing or redirecting the behavior. You may want to look at the topic paper in Section II entitled "What Is a Triggering Event?" Ask other family members or teachers if you want other opinions about what might be the purpose of a behavior. It is O.K. if you don't know. Perhaps the school autism consultant (if you have such access) can suggest possible purposes. By identifying the possible purpose, the respite worker may be able to draw upon his experience to deal with this situation with a different strategy than what you may recommend in the third column.

In the third column, list what effective strategies you use when each behavior occurs. Sometimes you use the same type of strategy for several different behaviors. See the list for Worksheet B-2 in this section and in the sample cases in (Section III). You will also use the information from Worksheet A to expand into Worksheets B-1 to B-3. On B-3, you will give recommendations for the order in which the respite worker should try the strategies and provide enough detail to insure sufficient understanding to allow implementation. Prepare Worksheet B-3 for only those behaviors that need this type of detail and ordering of strategies.

Ask for feedback after each respite visit so you know if you have provided enough guidance for respite workers or whether more information or detail is needed. Respite workers vary in terms of experience; over time, you will know what information to leave that will satisfy the needs of varying caregivers.

Worksheets B-1, B-2, and B-3

Each of these worksheets has been described in the preceding paragraphs. The explanation of strategies for Jon in B-1 was designed to give you an idea of what strategies might be called and how to describe them. B-2 lists all the strategies that you use to deal with all behaviors. You will use the same strategy more than once. While this provides good information for the respite worker, it doesn't tell her about what you have learned from experience with your child. That is why you will want to share information about which strategy to use first, when to switch to another strategy, and what makes a strategy successful. You could copy and paste content from B-2 to B-3 with your computer in instances where it will save you time. Blank copies are included in Section IV and on the computer disk. While the first preparation of Worksheets A, B-1, B-2, and B-3 will take some time, it shouldn't be too difficult to modify or update for future visits.

Sample of Worksheet A for Jon
The Summary

Behavior	Purposes	Strategy
Screaming	When makes a mistake	Relaxation; information about making mistakes
Avoidance of task	Wants to avoid making a mistake	Offer information: help available; when learning, people make mistakes If do X, then Y
Ignoring (when told to stop the computer)	Need to complete what he is doing	Timer; schedule; information about next opportunity
Laughing for what appears to be no reason	Amusing self; may be bored	Leave alone or check activity list
Cussing	Protesting	Acknowledge anger and ignore cussing; acknowledge and provide social information
Others ...	...	...

Sample of Worksheet B-1
Description of Problem Behaviors

- **Screaming** – Jon will yell at a moderate volume. Sometimes it is just angry sounds, at other times he may make angry statements. He will blame someone or something else for him making a mistake. Sometimes a cuss word is included in his tirade.

- **Avoidance of task** – Jon may walk away, not start a task or game, or push items away to avoid doing them. Sometimes he will tell you that he just doesn't want to do X.

- **Ignoring** – This may become an increasing strategy on his part as he gets older. He acts as if he has not heard what you have said. If he is immersed in a computer game, however, he may not hear someone's voice unless you "break the spell" for him.

- **Laughing for what appears to be no reason** – This upsets other people more than his family members because we are used to this behavior. Jon will replay favorite videos inside his head or think of funny things and laugh; he is unaware that others can hear and may think it is strange. He can get himself overstimulated, however. He will flap, make more noises and may jump around a bit when this occurs.

- **Cussing** – Jon has picked up some cuss words from his peers. His vocabulary is limited at this point. He doesn't know what the words mean or how others might interpret his comments. He sometimes uses these words when upset with himself or while interacting with others.

Sample of Worksheet B-2
Summary of Behavior Interventions Used with Jon

Ignoring physical actions – Do not give eye contact or look directly at Jon. Pretend you haven't noticed what he is doing.

Ignoring verbal responses – Continue the interaction and do not comment on behavior such as rudeness or cussing. If you are not in an interaction, ignore as described for a physical action.

Redirection – Direct or assist Jon to move on to another activity or to go to another location. The objective is to get his attention diverted from what we don't want him to do and redirected toward something more acceptable. Sometimes redirections are just reminders of what he needs to be doing. In other cases, the redirection is a distraction and has to be interesting enough to compete with what is currently the focus of his attention. For example, he may be redirected to playing with a favorite toy or going to his swing in the family room.

Timeout – Timeout is a removal from a troubling situation to a more sterile situation. Its purpose is to give Jon time to reflect about what he needs to do to be able to stay in a situation that he likes. It is not effective when the purpose of his behavior is to get away from an overstimulating situation. Timeout is not used often in our household since it doesn't teach Jon what he needs to do to be more effective.

Relaxation – Remove Jon from the overstimulating situation and present an alternative that he finds relaxing and calming. He may request a back rub or to go to his room.

Schedule information – When Jon needs to know if and when an event will happen or end, refer to the schedule in the kitchen. If the event is further removed in time, such as a vacation, refer to the monthly calendar that is hanging in the kitchen.

Timer – Use the timer when Jon needs to stay with a task for a certain amount of time or when something MUST terminate in a specific amount of time. A good example is our limit of 30 minutes for a bath.

Explanation or social/emotional information – Provide information in a concise, direct manner. For example, "It's very cold outside. No choice. You must wear a jacket. Me too." Or, if Jon tells someone to "shut up," tell Jon, "Saying 'shut up' was rude. People get angry at you. They don't like to hear 'shut up.' It is O.K. to nicely ask someone to be quieter. You can say, 'Can you be quieter, please? I'm trying to read my book.'"

Routine consequences – If Jon does something inappropriate, he must endure the natural consequences. For example, for deliberate pouring of milk on the floor, he must help wipe the milk up. If he gets chocolate on his shirt, he is to help soak the shirt in the sink to get it clean.

Visual support – Use a visual display of information such as a schedule, choice board, chart, pictures, gestures, sign language, and so forth. Visual displays are used to assist Jon to understand our verbal messages.

The best behavioral intervention is to adjust the environment to prevent the behavior from occurring.

Sample of Worksheet B-3
Order of Strategies for Specific Behaviors
(More Examples May Be Found in Section III)

Behavior #1: Screaming

More likely to occur when Jon has made a mistake.

Strategy #1 – Directive to relax and social information

Encourage Jon to take a deep breath, hold it while you count to five and then exhale. If he is cooperative, repeat five more times. Remind him that everyone makes mistakes and offer to help him fix the situation. (Or offer to rub his back to help calm him.)

Strategy #2 – Different directive to relax

Since Strategy #1 did not work, calmly direct Jon to go to his room, lie down on his bed and relax, or to go sit in the chair in the living room, family room, or porch if quiet and uninhabited. Tell him to come out when he is relaxed, and that you will talk about the problem later if he wants to do so. Gently guide him if he does not go on his own. Later, briefly talk about how to fix or avoid the problem, just like we discussed during your pre-respite visit. If it was an accident, remind him that "accidents happen."

Strategy #3 – More forceful directive to go relax

If he has failed to go, let him know that he needs to relax. Either he goes to his room by himself or you will need to lead him by the hand (OR he can choose something else from his relaxation list). He can decide, but he must relax. Count to ten and then help him if he is not moving. Later talk about it with him as much as possible with his language skills.

Behavior #2: Avoidance of task

Jon likes to be helpful, so it would be rare for him to refuse to do a task that he likes. He is more likely to refuse if a task is new or if he has made a mistake in the past.

Strategy #1 – Offer information

Provide information to help him decide if he can risk taking a chance on making a mistake. If the activity is a game of chance, remind him that he could win or lose the game but the idea is to have fun. Depending on what he is avoiding, provide information and allow him a little time to think about it, even if it is something that he must do (1 to 5 minutes is appropriate).

Strategy #2 – Offer help, if appropriate to the avoided task

Doing things together could be an option, if he is willing. If it is a game, consider skipping to strategy # 3.

Strategy #3 – Use an If-Then strategy

Give Jon some choices if this is not something that he must do: "If we begin to play the game and you want to stop, we will stop." Give him hints along the way if he is still learning the game: "If you don't want to play a game, let's choose something else."

Behavior #3: Laughing for no apparent reason

Strategy #1 – Ignoring

If the laughter is somewhat light and he is not getting too excited, it may be O.K. to ignore.

Strategy #2 – Redirection

If he is getting too stimulated or excited by his own self-amusement, redirect to another activity. Use the activity chart.

Behavior #4: Cussing

Strategies differ depending on whether Jon is cussing at you or if a few cuss words slip into his conversation. Cuss words are something new, so we are trying not to overreact and give him an excited response that will only increase the behavior.

Strategy #1 – Ignore and give information
Acknowledge that he is angry and what he is angry about. Try to focus on the problem; ignore the cuss words.

Strategy #2 – Give information
Acknowledge that he is angry but calmly let him know that he is being rude. Tell him he will need to tell you he is sorry, just like on "Nanny 911" (he has seen the show and he is aware of the apology part). If he doesn't, let him know that you will write this down on a memo pad for his Mom and then do so. If he apologizes, dramatically crumble up the paper and allow him to throw it away.

I-B: Day-of-the-Event Information

(Remember to prepare I-A first but I-B is likely to appear first in the notebook as shown in the case studies in Section III.)

L ife changes in little or major ways from day to day. These changes must be reflected in the Day-of-the-Event (I-B) Information. This is the section that will need updating or review *each time* there is a respite event. Not all pages will change.

This section discusses the following topics pages that require recent advance preparation for the respite worker:

- Emergency Information
- Permanent Contact List
- Today's Contact List
- The Flow of the Day
- The Schedule for Today
- Medications
- Activities for Today
- Food for Today
- Behavioral Challenges (repeat of Worksheets A, B-1, B-2 and B-3)

In Section III, you will find completed versions of these categories to guide you in making your own.

Emergency Information

This sheet may be located both in the notebook and near the phone. This is the key information that needs to be accessible for emergencies. Be sure to use your child's proper name so it can be matched against medical records, if necessary. See the case examples in Section III for ideas about what to include in terms of special warnings.

Permanent Contact List

This list includes all contacts and their phone numbers. This list can be prepared at the same time as Background, Section I-A, but it should be located with the I-B materials in the notebook.

Today's Contact List

Everyone on the Permanent Contact List will not be aware that you will be gone on a given day and, therefore, may not be available to help out if a problem arises. This specially prepared list identifies who is available that day and the order in which the care provider might try to call each party until someone can help.

The Flow of the Day

This form lets the respite person know who will be in or out at what point in the day. It also lets others know about setting events – things that might have happened earlier in the day or week that might impact your child's behavior. In addition, it alerts a returning respite worker as to what is new since his last visit.

Schedule for Today

Schedule for Today reflects your child's schedule. He may have a text- or picture-based copy of the same schedule. Be sure to show the worker how to make emergency changes on the schedule, if needed.

Medications

Generally, only list the medication that is likely to be given during the respite care. Go slightly beyond that deadline just in case you are unable to be home at the designated time and additional medication is taken soon after the deadline. Be sure the person knows where the medication is kept and how to deliver the prescribed dosage.

Activities for Today

These represent suggestions of possible activities to occur during the respite period. Your child may be able to suggest or select other appropriate activities, so these are backups. This decreases the chance that the respite worker is clueless about what to do and that your child will become upset by the innocent offer to do something that he hates.

With regard to video games, whether on a Gameboy™, Play Station™, or the computer, be sure to indicate if the current game can be paused or saved in memory. If the respite worker needs a demonstration of how to do this, do so, especially if your child is likely to be reluctant to stop when asked or at the designated time.

Food for the Day

This form presents menu information and acceptable food options as well as a list of what can *not* be eaten.

Behavioral Challenges

Place a duplicate copy of Worksheets A, B-1, B-2, and B-3 on behavior into this section. It is helpful for care providers to know in advance what strategies they might need to employ. Although this topic was arbitrarily put last in this section, a family may choose to put these sheets in the notebook right after the pages on Emergency Information. This information is put into both sections so that the respite worker can easily find it when a challenging situation arises.

Completing Section I-B

Begin working on the Day-of-the-Event (I-B) materials prior to the target date. The first time, beginning a week in advance might be advisable, but of course this depends on your personal schedule. Day-of-the-Event materials must be completed by the day of the respite service. Before arrival of the respite worker, give this section of material a final check for accuracy and completion, as things sometimes change rapidly in a busy household. This set of forms needs preparation and review each time a respite worker is used. Some sheets such as the Permanent Contact List only need a review for accuracy and changes. The others, such as Schedule of the Day, Foods for Today, and so forth, usually need to be constructed prior to each visit.

Note: It is also important to have these sheets prepared and handy when family members, friends, or neighbors provide respite support.

You will have a better sense of the time that goes into preparing for the respite worker after the first service. Recognize that for subsequent visits, you will be faster at creating the pages and may do a lot of cutting and pasting via your computer.

Where and How Should I Keep the Information for Respite Workers?

To keep everything together, consider using a notebook with section dividers marked appropriately so someone can quickly locate the desired information or review it upon arrival.

As shown in the case studies (Section III), consider using a larger font than the text on some of the pages. This will call attention to what you have written. Use highlighting as needed.

Information such as Food for the Day, Schedule, and Activities might be posted in a central location, such as the family bulletin board or the refrigerator, instead of or in addition to being in the notebook. The Permanent Contact List with phone numbers can be posted near a phone in addition to being included in the notebook. Some redundancy of important information is not a bad thing. Since things get misplaced easily in a busy household, consider keeping a backup copy in a specific place. (Always make sure to also update the backup copy.)

Section II
Information Sheets on Special Topics Related to Autism Spectrum Disorders

This section provides short papers on a variety of topics that may supplement the messages of parents to respite workers or other caregivers. The word "child" is used throughout the section since the primary user of this book will probably have a preschool- or school-age child who needs respite supervision. The selection of topics reflects the author's personal experiences with families and caregivers, as well as teachers and teaching assistants. Similar information will be relevant to respite providers. The print format ensures that the providers do not have to memorize all information but have something tangible that will provide an easy introduction or review of specific content.

Topics

- What Are Autism Spectrum Disorders or ASD?
- What Is ADD or ADHD?
- Why Doesn't the Child Look at Me?
- Why Should I Talk Slower or Use Pictures and Gestures, When Possible, When I Talk?
- Why Must I Be Careful About How Much or How I Talk?
- What Is Echolalia?
- What Is Augmentative and Alternative Communication (AAC)?
- What Is Picture Exchange Communication System, or PECS?
- Why Does This Child Talk on and on and On?
- What Are Sensory Issues?
- What Is a Schedule?
- What Is a Choice Board?
- What Are Routines, Predictability, and Structure?
- What Is a Triggering Event?
- What Is Positive Programming? Why Not Use Timeout or Some Type of Punishment?
- What Is a Prompt?
- Why Are Specific Foods on the Forbidden List?
- What Is Pica?
- Why Should I Be Concerned About What Jewelry and Clothing I Wear?

What Are Autism Spectrum Disorders or ASD?

Autism spectrum disorders is a term used to cover a range of diagnostic categories that share common characteristics, including autism, Asperger Syndrome, and pervasive developmental disorder, not otherwise specified (PDD-NOS).

The child with a diagnosis of autism usually demonstrates, in terms of number, the most characteristic differences when young. The child with PDD-NOS has the least number of obvious characteristics. The commonality between all three categories is a neurological basis for difficulties in

- social interaction
- communication
- restricted, repetitive behaviors or restricted interests.

Children with ASD do not have common specific physical features, such as found in Down's syndrome, for example. Often these children are very attractive in appearance. Their major differences relate to temperament, abilities, and interests. For example, some children with autism and PDD-NOS have cognitive limitations (what used to be called mild, moderate, or severe/profound mental retardation). Some children from all categories are very intelligent. A few selective common characteristics for all three diagnostic categories of ASD are listed in the following table.

B. Vicker, *Sharing Information About Your Child with an Autism Spectrum Disorder*, 2007. Shawnee Mission, KS: Autism Asperger Publishing Company, www.asperger.net

Characteristic	Example of Characteristic
Social Interaction	• May have limited interest in others • May not understand that others interpret actions or events differently from him
Communication	• May only communicate to get needs met, if cued or highly motivated • May have limited understanding of the language used by others
Repetitive Behaviors, Restricted Interests	• May engage in hand flicking for stimulation or to reduce stress • May only want to talk about topics of personal interest

The disorder is lifelong and is *not* caused by poor or ineffective parenting. There seems to be a genetic basis for many instances of the disorder. Extensive research is being conducted to help everyone better understand the disorder and to suggest more effective strategies for helping individuals develop, learn, and be successful.

It is difficult to give sufficient information about this complex disorder within a short handout. Interested caregivers may want to read other material and view videos on the topic. Ask the family for additional references.

B. Vicker, *Sharing Information About Your Child with an Autism Spectrum Disorder*, 2007. Shawnee Mission, KS: Autism Asperger Publishing Company, www.asperger.net

What Is ADD or ADHD?

Sometimes individuals with ASD are diagnosed with a different disability before the pattern of ASD is recognized. For example, many who have average or above-average intellectual abilities are initially diagnosed with attention deficit disorder (ADD) or with attention deficit hyperactivity disorder (ADHD). For some, the ADD or ADHD diagnosis gets dropped and is replaced by a diagnosis of ASD; others may be diagnosed as having both disorders.

According to the website of the Children and Adults with Attention Deficit Hyperactivity Disorder (CHADD; http://www.chadd.org/), ADHD is the official term for this disability. Like ASD, it has three different subtypes, one with a hyperactive-impulsive component, another with inattention, and a third with a combination of the first two. The main characteristics are:

- Distractibility (e.g., difficulty keeping attention focused on a task such as homework; poor organizational skills such as keeping track of homework assignments).
- Impulsivity (e.g., blurts out answers before questions have been completed; difficulty waiting to taking turns).
- Hyperactivity (excessive activity and physical restlessness; e.g., difficulty keeping one's body at rest during class or mealtime).

To qualify for a diagnosis of ADHD, the behaviors, according to CHADD, must be excessive, last longer than six months, occur before an individual is seven years of age and "create a real handicap in at least two areas of the person's life such as school, home, work, or social settings."

When dealing with a child with ADHD, it can be deceiving to watch the child being very intensely focused for long periods of time on specific favorite activities and yet have very little patience or attention for non-

B. Vicker, *Sharing Information About Your Child with an Autism Spectrum Disorder*, 2007. Shawnee Mission, KS: Autism Asperger Publishing Company, www.asperger.net

favorite tasks. In other words, the lack of attention does not apply to all situations; only some.

Many children with ASD show some of the characteristics of ADHD, including poor judgment, poor organizational skills, especially with school assignments, and restlessness. Whether the child with ASD has a second disability depends on the severity and persistence of the symptoms. A diagnosis of ADHD is made by a psychologist, psychiatrist, or a medical doctor.

If a child has the ADHD diagnosis, the caregiver must provide close supervision. Regardless of the child's age or intellectual abilities, he may impulsively do or say things that could put himself and others in danger. Even without ADHD, the child with ASD often has no realistic fear or awareness of dangerous situations, so close supervision by adults is crucial. The parents will advise you about this additional disorder if it is diagnosed or suspected. They should also provide information about what behavior the child might engage in and how to best manage or redirect the behavior. Ensuring safety is paramount.

B. Vicker, *Sharing Information About Your Child with an Autism Spectrum Disorder*, 2007. Shawnee Mission, KS: Autism Asperger Publishing Company, www.asperger.net

Why Doesn't the Child Look at Me?

One of the main characteristics of ASD is difficulty in social interactions. Difficulty with eye contact is related to problems with social interaction. There may be several reasons why the child is not looking at you when you talk to him:

- The child may understand little of what you say and consequently have little interest in the words that are coming out of your mouth.
- The child may not have learned that giving eye contact, at least fleetingly, is the social or polite thing to do. (Children without ASD usually look at you automatically without having to be taught.)
- The child may not know that your facial expression adds meaning to your words and that, therefore, it is important to look at your face.
- The child may find it difficult to look at your whole face and may only be able to look at a specific part or look toward you but not at you. Looking at your face may produce sensory overload; he may experience too much information or too many movements to be able to process at the same time.
- The child may find it too difficult to look at your face, listen to your message, and try to put together some answer all at the same time. By not looking at you, it is easier for the child to focus on the message exchange, and thus reduce the multitasking that must be done.

Check with the parents to learn if you are to require the child to look toward you when you talk to him. Some children are at a stage where they are learning this social behavior; others may not be ready for this social demand.

Also check with the parents to learn if the child is usually listening if you have called her name but are not getting eye contact. Sometimes the child is listening and you can go ahead and give directions. Other times, it may be necessary to get near the child, call her name, tap the shoulder, and give the directive again.

B. Vicker, *Sharing Information About Your Child with an Autism Spectrum Disorder*, 2007. Shawnee Mission, KS: Autism Asperger Publishing Company, www.asperger.net

Why Should I Talk Slower and Use Pictures and Gestures, When Possible, When I Talk?

All individuals with ASD have some difficulties with comprehension. How much difficulty and how consistently depends on the individual and factors such as age, experience, and circumstance. For example, young children may have more difficulty understanding the speech of others than would adults with ASD.

The analogy of a foreigner visiting our country is often used to help others understand the language comprehension difficulties of individuals with ASD. If you were talking to someone from another country, you would do some of the following to help him understand your message.

- *You would talk slower* so that the person can hear all of your words and be more aware of the sentence pattern and word endings. (Many individuals with ASD have difficulty processing rapid speech.)

- *You would use some gesture* so the person might know what you are talking about. This is only possible when you are talking about a person or an object in the immediate vicinity. You can point to or tap the table in question, for example. Young children may not be good at following the direction of a pointed finger. The young child may look at your finger rather than follow the direction to a specific object. For very young children you may need to actually touch the object.

- *You might show a picture* of the object or place that you are talking about. Many young children, in particular, have a poor understanding of syntax or how sentences are constructed. The longer the sentence, the more the child is likely to tune into only a few words. If a child only tunes into a single word that he recognizes, he might get a different meaning and expectation than you intend-

B. Vicker, *Sharing Information About Your Child with an Autism Spectrum Disorder*, 2007. Shawnee Mission, KS: Autism Asperger Publishing Company, www.asperger.net

ed. For example, if you said, "Your mom needs to go to the store to buy more cookies," your hope is that the child will understand that you are out of cookies and, therefore, not want more cookies. However, if he only tunes into a primary word, which for him is "cookies," he will be expecting cookies to appear and might be upset when they don't. A photo of the grocery store might shift the focus of his thinking.

- *You would also keep your sentences short, repeat the meaning in another sentence, and watch your vocabulary and the use of figurative language.* Figurative language refers to phrases that are figures of speech and not representative of what the words might suggest. Examples include "raining cats and dogs," "shake a leg," "mom is feeling blue today," where the real meaning is "It's raining hard," "Hurry up," and "Mom is feeling sad today."

If you keep the analogy of a foreigner in mind, it might be easier to communicate with children who have certain language/comprehension problems. The payoff for you could be a more cooperative child and an easier childcare experience as effective communication is essential for successful personal interactions.

B. Vicker, *Sharing Information About Your Child with an Autism Spectrum Disorder*, 2007. Shawnee Mission, KS: Autism Asperger Publishing Company, www.asperger.net

Why Must I Be Careful About How Much or How I Talk?

Children with ASD often have difficulties in the area of social relationships and understanding language. If the child is exposed to too much talking, he might:

- Tune out or not listen to all of your messages. The child may not be able to pick out what is important or know how to respond.
- Be overwhelmed and become irritable or confused. This could lead to aggression, behavioral outbursts, or a desire to withdraw to a quieter place.
- Be unable to process all the information and only process and respond to a few key words, or what he may have thought you said. Your sentences may have been too long and difficult to follow.
- Be unable to process fast enough because the message is coming too rapidly without enough pausing. This could lead to a feeling of failure and increasing irritability.
- Be unable to filter out your message from the background noise.

In general, it is better to talk when necessary than to chat on and on. Often people talk a lot when they are nervous; many people in our culture feel uncomfortable when there is extended silence. Many children with autism welcome silence; indeed, they prefer it.

When you speak to the child, consider the following:

- Get the child's attention before talking. She may be listening even if she does not look at you. (Check with the parents for guidance.)
- Speak at a slower-than-normal pace.
- Keep your sentences short and the grammar simple, and use familiar vocabulary.

B. Vicker, *Sharing Information About Your Child with an Autism Spectrum Disorder*, 2007. Shawnee Mission, KS: Autism Asperger Publishing Company, www.asperger.net

- Point, gesture, use pictures or a manual sign to focus the child's attention on the important part of your message, if the parents report that this is helpful.
- Try to eliminate competing background noise when you are talking (others talking, the TV on, music playing, etc.).

Some children with very good or sensitive hearing are bothered if someone talks in a loud manner; to this child, the loud talking may be experienced as someone shouting at him. Other children are bothered by a voice that is too bouncy, too high-pitched, or too shrill. Some will ignore a voice that is too soft or too low in volume. The parents will be able to provide guidance relative to the special needs and preferences of their child.

B. Vicker, *Sharing Information About Your Child with an Autism Spectrum Disorder*, 2007. Shawnee Mission, KS: Autism Asperger Publishing Company, www.asperger.net

What Is Echolalia?

Echolalia is a term used to describe a pattern of vocalization often used by young children with ASD. Echolalia refers to an echoing or repetition of sounds or speech. The echoing may be the duplication of sounds such as the dog barking or the hum of the fluorescent light. Usually the echoing represents the speech of others from real life, TV shows, commercials, videos, or music. Older children and adults may also exhibit echolalia.

There are two main types of echolalia: immediate and delayed. *Immediate echolalia* is a repetition of something that was just spoken or sung. For example, if a mother asked her child, "Do you want juice?" the child might repeat the sentence back, "Do you want juice?" as he grabs some juice. In this case the child was using the echo to say "yes." A few days later, the child might go up to his mom, tug at her slacks and say, "Let's do the Dew" to indicate that he wants something to drink. He wasn't really asking for Mountain Dew soda or trying to be funny or cute. He was using something that he memorized from a TV commercial to try to let his mom know that he was thirsty. This is an example of *delayed echolalia*.

Why do some children and adults with ASD repeat or echo the speech of others? Because ...
- They do not understand the individual words and sentence patterns used, and they repeat a whole sentence as if it were a single vocabulary word.
- They are not able to make their own unique sentences.
- When they are stressed or anxious, they have difficulty putting their own thoughts into unique words and sentences, so they use phrases that they have stored in their memory.

B. Vicker, *Sharing Information About Your Child with an Autism Spectrum Disorder*, 2007. Shawnee Mission, KS: Autism Asperger Publishing Company, www.asperger.net

Some children with ASD never move into the stage of using echolalia; others never move out of that stage. Still others move on to use unique sentences much or most of the time. It is much more difficult to recognize the use of echolalia in a child who also can make up his own sentences. The cue for identifying echoing might be that the child is using words or sentences that sound a little unusual for the situation or appear to be fairly sophisticated relative to the child's typical language patterns. As the child gets older and develops better skills, it is often more difficult to recognize that she is really repeating some dialogue from the TV because she may be using it in a fairly appropriate manner. After repeated contact with a child and her favorite videos, it will be easier to recognize repetitive or echoed use of certain phrases.

It is important to remember the following about echolalia:
- The child may not be able to express his message in a better way than echoed speech.
- The child probably can't tell you what the actual message is. So if you don't understand the echolalia, it is probably not helpful to ask for clarification.
- Do not take echoed speech as a cue about the child's level of understanding about a situation. Frequently, children use words or phrases that they don't understand. Their echolalia must be interpreted with respect, but also with caution.

Get guidance from the parents. They can tell you if and how their child uses echolalia.

B. Vicker, *Sharing Information About Your Child with an Autism Spectrum Disorder*, 2007. Shawnee Mission, KS: Autism Asperger Publishing Company, www.asperger.net

What Is Augmentative and Alternative Communication (AAC)?

Augmentative and alternative communication (AAC) refers to a variety of means of communication that can be used to substitute or supplement oral speech. Users of AAC include the following:

- Adults or children who have not learned how to talk
- Adults or children who are unable to talk
- Adults or children who talk but whose speech is not understandable to most people
- Adults or children who primarily echo words and are not able to express their unique messages
- Adults or children who have some speech but not enough to meet daily needs
- Adults or children who have some degree of speech but are unable to put together appropriate spoken messages when they are highly anxious, stressed, or agitated

Some individuals use AAC for most of their communication situations. Others only need to use AAC techniques under certain circumstances.

AAC covers a wide range of intervention options. A child might need to learn gestures such as a negative headshake, pointing, or taking someone by the hand and going to the area where their desired "goodies" are kept. A child might learn some sign language for specific messages such as "break," "help," and "more," or might learn to exchange a picture for a desired item or point to a picture on a display. Another option is to depress a button on an electronic communication device that announces a chosen message. Children who can spell might use text in handwritten form or use a computer to generate messages.

An individual's program may contain a variety of approaches or tools, and

B. Vicker, *Sharing Information About Your Child with an Autism Spectrum Disorder*, 2007. Shawnee Mission, KS: Autism Asperger Publishing Company, www.asperger.net

these may change as the child develops more skills and experiences different demands for communication. It is important to know what the child uses and how to support it.

A limited example of what is called a topic board is provided below. The sample topic board might be used as an AAC support while reading a book to a child.

Topic Board

Mommy (photo of Mom)	Read book	Read again (or use manual sign)	I like the book	Different book
Daddy (photo of Dad)	Make sounds (of animals)	I turn page	I don't like it	All done (or manual sign for "finished") THE END

This type of a display allows the child to (a) ask a specific parent to read to her, (b) signal that she would like a different book, (c) request that she be allowed to turn the pages, and (d) request to terminate the book at the natural ending or some time in between and do so in a socially acceptable manner. These messages give the child some power in the reading situation and also encourage interaction.

AAC offers powerful tools to foster communication skills. It is easier to use these tools if you understand their purpose and how to use them. Be sure to ask for guidance.

B. Vicker, *Sharing Information About Your Child with an Autism Spectrum Disorder*, 2007. Shawnee Mission, KS: Autism Asperger Publishing Company, www.asperger.net

What Is the Picture Exchange Communication System, or PECS?

The Picture Exchange Communication System, or PECS, is a form of augmentative communication that works well with many children with ASD. It represents a beginning system of communication and usually involves using pictures as symbols for the objects desired by the person with ASD. There are six specific steps in the total program, and procedures vary by the step. It is important to get instructions and training from the parents if the child is to use this means of communication during their absence.

Depending on the age of any other children or adults in the environment, your role may be that of the *communication partner* (i.e., the one who gets the message and acts on it) or that of the *facilitator* (i.e., the person who cues the child to grab the picture to make an exchange). The parents will make suggestions for your role.

In Stages I and II of the PECS program, the communication partner shows the child something that she likes. The child's job is to grab the one and only picture on the top of a notebook and give it to the communication partner. If she doesn't, the second person, the facilitator, helps the child pick up the picture card from the notebook on the table and make the exchange. The facilitator does not talk to the child; he is a silent helper.

It is important to carry out each stage correctly as the child might otherwise learn a wrong habit. There are correction procedures for teaching, but this is probably not something a parent would ask a respite worker to do.

The picture used by the child may be a photograph or a line drawing. Below are some examples of commonly used items that children often wish

B. Vicker, *Sharing Information About Your Child with an Autism Spectrum Disorder*, 2007. Shawnee Mission, KS: Autism Asperger Publishing Company, www.asperger.net

to request. An easy way is to generate pictures is to use a software program called Boardmaker™ by Mayer Johnson (http://www.mayer-johnson.com/). For some children, however, these pictures are too abstract, making it necessary to use other visual symbols such as photographs.

| Juice | Pretzel | Puzzle | Book | Popsicle |

Usually the single pictures are mounted on poster board, laminated, or covered with clear contact paper with a Velcro mount on the back. Once the child is beyond the first few stages, he should be able to find the picture in the notebook on his own and give it to you.

Treat the symbol given to you as a request. Like all requests from children, however, some cannot be honored. Let the parents guide you in terms of how to respond to requests made with the PECS material. They may have a way of showing the child in a visual format that a request cannot be met at the moment. Often this is an X symbol much like the symbol used to tell you "no parking."

Being aware of the child's communication system is important. Not only does this promote a more positive relationship with him, but it also reduces the opportunity for an outburst or negative behavior due to failure to communicate and get his needs met.

B. Vicker, *Sharing Information About Your Child with an Autism Spectrum Disorder*, 2007. Shawnee Mission, KS: Autism Asperger Publishing Company, www.asperger.net

Why Does This Child Talk on and on and On?

Many people who have had no personal experience with children with ASD have the impression that the children do not want to be around others and are quite silent. It can be a shock, then, to meet a child with Asperger Syndrome (one of the categories of ASD) who wants to talk on and on about his favorite topic. It is important to understand this type of child who seems to contradict your expectations.

This child initially seems to have no problem with communication, yet he has significant problems. These problems include:

- Difficulty conversing about topics other than those of his own interest. He may not know what to say about other topics. On the other hand, he may have read and memorized volumes about a particular topic of interest, such as volcanoes.
- Difficulty understanding the rules of conversation. The child may not realize that you and he are to take turns talking. Often the child carries on a monologue or a solitary conversation.
- Difficulty understanding that a conversation does not consist of a recitation of facts. People typically add comments, ask questions, seek clarification, and so on, so there is a back-and-forth development to the conversation.
- Difficulty understanding that you may not be interested in his topic. Effective conversations must be about mutually agreed upon topics by both partners, or at least involve turn taking.
- Difficulty reading your facial expression and body language signaling that you are uncomfortable with the situation and may want to stop the conversation. For example, he may not notice that you are slowly trying to back away or that your face has an anxious or very neutral appearance.

B. Vicker, *Sharing Information About Your Child with an Autism Spectrum Disorder*, 2007. Shawnee Mission, KS: Autism Asperger Publishing Company, www.asperger.net

- Difficulty knowing how to terminate a conversation. After he has finished the monologue, he may just turn around and walk away. This behavior is less objectionable in a young child, but is inappropriate for a teenager or young adult.
- Difficulty knowing the true purpose of a social interaction. The child may ask a routine set of questions instead of a monologue, but seem very disinterested in your answers. He may be more interested in (a) completing the questions, (b) wanting to see if your answers are the same as those of others he has asked, (c) wanting to establish an opportunity to show off that only he knows the answer to his questions, or (d) engaging in a variety of other behaviors that appear to have a hidden purpose.

If you understand some of the reasons for what is happening, you will be better able to listen and view the situation as the child tries to interact with you. If you need to set a cutoff point, tell the child he can talk about his topic for five more minutes and then must stop. It may seem rude, but sometimes it is a necessary action.

B. Vicker, *Sharing Information About Your Child with an Autism Spectrum Disorder*, 2007. Shawnee Mission, KS: Autism Asperger Publishing Company, www.asperger.net

What Are Sensory Issues?

Many children with ASD have sensory issues. This means that their sense of sight, hearing, taste, smell, touch, and/or perception of their body in space operates differently than what is experienced by most children and adults. Sensory issues are not exclusive to autism and can be found with other disabilities and in the typical population. Some individuals with autism are at the more extreme end of the range of difficulty, however.

Although there is a common pattern to these issues, the type and severity differ between individuals. The following list only mentions some common sensory-based behaviors.

Sensory issues can include any of the following:

- Oversensitivity or hypersensitivity to certain stimuli sensations that is markedly different from what is experienced by most people. The child might experience pain, discomfort, or anxiety when areas of hypersensitivity are affected. These areas might include the following:
    - Sensitivity to *touch*, including hair combing, teeth brushing, the feel of specific fabrics on the skin, the temperature of water or the weather, being touched or bumped by others in a crowd, or having others in close proximity. The child may need lots of personal space and desensitization (exposure in small steps) to help him tolerate necessary contact with certain materials and people.
    - Sensitivity to *sound*, including magnification of the hum of fluorescent lights, ordinary conversation, and environmental sounds. The child may need earplugs, a masking sound produced by an air purifier or music on a Walkman, iPod™, or removal from the offending environment.

B. Vicker, *Sharing Information About Your Child with an Autism Spectrum Disorder*, 2007. Shawnee Mission, KS: Autism Asperger Publishing Company, www.asperger.net

- Sensitivity to *visual* stimuli, including sunlight, ordinary light, or the sight of many visual stimuli within a setting, such as the brightly decorated grocery store, the many colors of flowers and play equipment outside in the yard, or his sister's colorful room with numerous posters, mobiles, and material flowing from the canopy top of her bed. The child may need sunglasses, reduced lighting, and/or exposure to a less stimulating environment.
  - Sensitivity to *food textures*; may only eat specific types of foods. Specific programming can help broaden the diet.

- Undersensitivity or hyposensitivity to certain sensations either most of the time or upon occasion. The same child may be hypersensitive at some times and hyposensitive at others. Areas of undersensitivity may include the following:
  - Reduced sensitivity to *sound*, particularly speech. Parents may have wondered if the child was deaf.
  - Reduced responsiveness to *stimuli associated with an activity*. The child may need intense stimulation to get aroused from passivity to activity or interaction. Sometimes this arousal will take the form of a very active movement such as swinging or jumping.
  - Reduced sensitivity to *pain and temperature*. The child may show no or reduced reaction to cuts, fractures, or general pain. The child may not flinch if he puts his hand into hot water or touches a hot stove.

- An attraction or need for certain types of stimuli. This might include:
  - Increased attraction to *visual stimuli* such as watching a flag waving in the wind, water circling in a toilet bowl, scraps of paper falling like confetti, or looking at letter or number configurations in print or on the TV screen.
  - Increased need to touch certain types of hair, clothing, or objects.

B. Vicker, *Sharing Information About Your Child with an Autism Spectrum Disorder*, 2007. Shawnee Mission, KS: Autism Asperger Publishing Company, www.asperger.net

       ○ Increased need for auditory input. The child may engage in echolalic repetition of memorized dialogue or song lyrics directed to him.

- A need for movement such as swinging, rocking, or pacing to aid calming.
- A need for a certain type of pressure upon the body to aid calming.

The parent will provide you with specific information about sensory issues and how to manage them. Accommodating the child's issues will help him remain more calm and relaxed.

B. Vicker, *Sharing Information About Your Child with an Autism Spectrum Disorder*, 2007. Shawnee Mission, KS: Autism Asperger Publishing Company, www.asperger.net

What Is a Schedule?

A schedule is a visual listing of events in the order in which they will happen. A schedule may consist of a list using text or printed words, a list of pictures, or a list of pictures accompanied by text. Below is an example of a family schedule for a Saturday morning using pictures and text.

Eat breakfast	
Get dressed	
Go to library	
Get gas for car	
Swing at park	

B. Vicker, *Sharing Information About Your Child with an Autism Spectrum Disorder*, 2007. Shawnee Mission, KS: Autism Asperger Publishing Company, www.asperger.net

Schedules allow the child to know what is going to happen and in what order, thereby putting predictability into her life – an important requirement for children with ASD. For example, she will know that mom must go to the library and buy gas before she gets to go the park. With a visual schedule, the child is less likely to forget that getting gas has to occur before playing in the park. The visual schedule may prevent confusion, misunderstanding and, ultimately, a behavioral outburst.

Children with ASD tend to be visual learners; that is; they tend to learn better from seeing how things work than from hearing about them. Schedules can help a child cope with change and prepare herself to leave one situation and move onto another. For example, if she is bothered by music blaring at the gas station, the child can be reminded that she will only be there for a few minutes. She can cover her ears or listen to a Walkman with her preferred music during the uncomfortable situation. She will also know that something good will happen after the more difficult situation (i.e., she will get to go to the park and swing).

Ultimately, schedules are important tools in helping children self-manage their behavior and often become a strategy used as part of an overall positive behavior plan (i.e., used to reduce the likelihood of outbursts when information is lacking about what will happen next). A schedule is particularly important during a respite stay in order to help foster a sense of security and predictability for the child. It will make the stay more pleasant for both you and the child.

B. Vicker, *Sharing Information About Your Child with an Autism Spectrum Disorder*, 2007. Shawnee Mission, KS: Autism Asperger Publishing Company, www.asperger.net

What Is a Choice Board?

A choice board is a visual display or support that may contain pictures or words. The choice board is, as its name suggests, a way of showing someone what his choices are. Children with ASD do not always process information as you do. The information may come too fast or they may be thinking about the first choice offered and, therefore, fail to listen to the other option(s).

A visual display offers the following advantages:

- All choices are shown at once; therefore, the ability to remember all the choices is not an issue.
- The child has time to consider the options without forgetting the alternatives while trying to make a decision.
- The child's response is clear when he points to a choice (the choice may not have been clear if the child had to use his speaking ability).

Choice boards may be permanent or changeable. Although the examples that follow involve food, choice displays can display options such as book, videos, or activity selections. In some situations, there may be a limited set of choices and a permanent display may be used (i.e., the pictures or words don't change). For example, outside of mealtimes, the choices for beverage may be water or iced tea; otherwise, a child might drink a lot of juice that may reduce his appetite for mealtime food. In other situations, the display must be able to be changed perhaps several times a day, or, there may be multiple choice boards to meet specific purposes. For example, if a choice of milk or juice is offered at lunch, some type of fruit and cracker may be available for an afternoon snack and popcorn or ice cream is offered as an evening snack. The changeable display may have one type of Velcro tabs (the flat, sticky loop) and the choice cards, the opposite Velcro tabs (the thicker, soft hook). See the following example for a changeable activity board.

B. Vicker, *Sharing Information About Your Child with an Autism Spectrum Disorder*, 2007. Shawnee Mission, KS: Autism Asperger Publishing Company, www.asperger.net

Choice Board for "Next Activity"

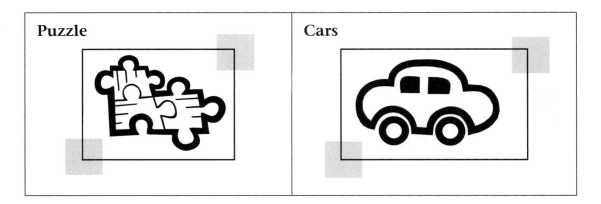

| Puzzle | Cars |

It is important to understand what choice boards do for the child with ASD. Using choice boards is part of managing behavior. Offering choice provides a child with ASD some control in a situation; some children with ASD have a strong need for control. Using a choice board can prevent a problem behavior or outburst from occurring. It is easy to use a choice board. It will be much more stressful and time consuming to deal with a behavior problem that occurs because you did not take the time to use the choice board.

B. Vicker, *Sharing Information About Your Child with an Autism Spectrum Disorder*, 2007. Shawnee Mission, KS: Autism Asperger Publishing Company, www.asperger.net

What Are Routines, Predictability and Structure? Why Are They Important?

Routines are established ways of doing things. Everyone has routines. It makes life easier if we don't have to plan out the steps or sequence for routine things on a daily basis. Thus, routines allow us to save mental energy for more unique tasks. For example, the family may have a certain routine for going to bed at night. Events happen in a certain sequence, and within that sequence there are various subroutines for getting undressed, playing in the tub, getting dressed for bed, reading a story, saying "good night," and staying in bed. Sometimes the routine or subroutine is established by the child, and the adult incorporates the child's routine into the household routine.

Once established, routines foster *predictability,* and predictability fosters comfort. Routines can be identified on schedules. A visual display offers a concrete way of showing what is expected to occur as well as any changes in routine. Children with ASD often organize their world in terms of routines. As a result, when a routine is violated and predictability has failed, the child can become unhappy, confused, and anxious. For example, Jon routinely eats breakfast before getting dressed in the morning. If the routine is reversed, he may worry while getting dressed whether he will eat breakfast or not.

Structure refers to the organization of time, environment, and activities of daily life. If you stick somewhat closely to a schedule, you are providing structure for the child. If there is limited predictability and no established routines, the environment would be called unstructured, and the child may pace the room, rock his body, and become visibly anxious.

Children with ASD thrive on routine, predictability and structure. This is important to remember as it enables you to have a more successful experience with the child.

B. Vicker, *Sharing Information About Your Child with an Autism Spectrum Disorder,* 2007. Shawnee Mission, KS: Autism Asperger Publishing Company, www.asperger.net

What Is a Triggering Event?

Sometimes taking care of a child with ASD can be confusing. This is particularly true when something otherwise ordinary becomes a triggering event. The meaning of this term may be more obvious after reading the following example situation.

*Jon is usually very cooperative about most things, but today he exploded into angry yelling and stomping of his feet when his mom asked him to hang up his jacket after playing outside. The act of asking him to hang up the jacket may have been a triggering event. On most days, he would willingly hang up his jacket on the hook in the laundry room. Today, however, he may have had some experiences that progressively increased his stress level until he blew. For example, he may not have had enough sleep last night, his body was adjusting to new medication, it was cold outside so he could only play on the playground for a short time, he didn't get to swing, which is his favorite sensory activity, and his hat felt scratchy on his head. Add all of this together and the child had a high level of frustration and irritability **before** he was asked to take off his jacket. Tomorrow he may be totally cooperative about taking off the jacket, but today was different.*

All the things that happened to Jon before the request about hanging up his jacket are called "setting events" because they set the stage for something to happen. Losing control in a given moment happens to everyone, including people with ASD. Many people are able to identify what may have irritated them before they exploded over something minor. The child with ASD has difficulty being that reflective. Until Jon can recognize the signs indicating that his irritability is growing and that he may need to do something to calm himself, minor events can set off more explosive reactions.

B. Vicker, *Sharing Information About Your Child with an Autism Spectrum Disorder*, 2007. Shawnee Mission, KS: Autism Asperger Publishing Company, www.asperger.net

Usually there are signs that a child is getting irritated. Some may pace back and forth more, make more vocal noises, do lots of heavy breathing, flap, rock, or echo more phrases. It is at this point that someone can help. The child may need to do something that is more relaxing such as sitting in a bean bag chair, wrapping a blanket around his body, getting rid of some energy by jumping on a mini-trampoline, going for a walk, or a similar activity.

Doing this type of analysis and early intervention is part of positive programming. The parents may leave you guideline strategies about what works best for their child, or they may leave a choice board (see page 96) that depicts what frequently helps with calming down; the child will choose what she thinks will work best for her in that moment.

The bottom line is that if a child performs an action (such as hanging up his coat after entering the house) most days but explodes once in a while, that situation may be acting as a triggering event. It is the last straw in the chain of bad events. Triggering events, while unpleasant, are like red flags saying "take notice and help me."

B. Vicker, *Sharing Information About Your Child with an Autism Spectrum Disorder*, 2007. Shawnee Mission, KS: Autism Asperger Publishing Company, www.asperger.net

What Is Positive Programming? Why Not Use Timeout or Some Type of Punishment?

Many people have been taught that the way to change a "bad" behavior is to punish a child; timeout is often viewed as a punishment technique.* Many parents have tried punishment interventions with their child with ASD and generally have not been very successful. Instead, their child often still engages in the "bad" behavior such as yelling, screaming, hitting, and so forth. The practical question to ask is, "Why doesn't punishment work for these children?"

Punishment doesn't always work because it doesn't teach the child how to get her needs met in a more socially acceptable way. For example, if the child is over-stimulated by the commotion of a typical household, she may begin screaming. She may not know how or be able to tell her mom that she needs to go to her room and have some quiet time. Putting her in timeout doesn't teach her an acceptable way of asking to go to her room, but it may actually help her achieve what she needs. In fact, she may have learned that screaming may be a good way for her to get access to quiet because it is an aspect of timeout. In this case, screaming will probably occur more often than less when she is overstimulated. In other words, the child is learning that she gets her needs met (i.e., quiet), if she screams. This was not the parent's intention.

To avoid similar situations, families might try positive programming. The objective of positive programming is to avoid, in this case, the screaming behavior. The family will be more careful about how much stimulation

---

* *Timeout is an effective intervention strategy from the standpoint of decreasing a behavior only if the child dislikes being removed from a situation and wants to quickly get back to it. This is not the case with a child who is craving removal from stimulation. This child may want the timeout to last a long time because it makes him feel better (i.e., more relaxed).*

B. Vicker, *Sharing Information About Your Child with an Autism Spectrum Disorder*, 2007. Shawnee Mission, KS: Autism Asperger Publishing Company, www.asperger.net

their daughter experiences and intervene before screaming begins. The child might also be taught to express her need for quiet by saying something or by giving someone a picture card that requests going to a quiet place. This latter approach might not eliminate screaming 100 percent, but should reduce it while also teaching the child a useful lifelong skill; for example, that socially acceptable communication can also get her what she wants or needs.

Depending on individual needs, positive programming might include:
- Providing a means to communicate specific messages.
- Providing certain sensory experiences.
- Avoiding certain sensory experiences.
- Teaching a child how to relax when she is tense or anxious.
- Providing information about what is going to happen next by using a schedule or verbal information.
- Providing choices.
- Providing a child with opportunities to expend energy.
- Providing a child with opportunities to help others.

If one understands the principles behind positive programming (i.e., the prevention of behavior problems), it is easier to follow through with family requests to do certain things, including using choice boards, schedules, and such.

B. Vicker, *Sharing Information About Your Child with an Autism Spectrum Disorder*, 2007. Shawnee Mission, KS: Autism Asperger Publishing Company, www.asperger.net

What Is a Prompt?

A prompt is a technique used to help a child or adult successfully perform a task. Essentially, prompts are cues to help a person perform some action or to help a person remember something. For many children with ASD, prompts are often an important and necessary part of learning certain new skills. They take many forms and have special names. For example, a prompt for repositioning a puzzle piece might be:

- A word or a phrase such as "turn it" (a verbal prompt).
- A gesture such as pointing, or body movement that suggests turning (a visual prompt).
- A sign from sign language that means "turn" (a visual prompt).
- A nudge at the child's elbow to suggest he needs to move his hand (a physical prompt).
- Hand-over-hand assistance to turn the puzzle piece and insert it into the puzzle frame (physical assistance).
- A demonstration of part of or the entire desired action (modeling).
- A picture that suggests turning or the printed phrase "turn it" (a visual prompt).

Prompts are positive cues when they are used to foster success and independence in performing an action. They are negative cues when they encourage dependence. The family will be the best source of information about what types of prompts the child needs, how often they are needed, and under what circumstances they need to be provided.

It is important to remember:

- Parents try to avoid accidentally teaching their child to be prompt-dependent. They do not want their child to learn to wait for someone to cue him about what to do each time an action must be performed. As a care provider, this may mean that you give the child a

B. Vicker, *Sharing Information About Your Child with an Autism Spectrum Disorder*, 2007. Shawnee Mission, KS: Autism Asperger Publishing Company, www.asperger.net

chance to do something by herself first before prompting. The parents can tell you how long you might wait before prompting. For example, the parents may tell you to silently count to 30 to allow time for the child to perform a needed action on her own.

- Give the best prompt according to the parents' suggestion. Because verbal prompts are the easiest and most natural, you may be tempted to use this type as a first choice. For a variety of reasons, the parents may want you to use one of the other types first.
- Don't give too many prompts in a short period of time. The child with ASD may get overwhelmed. Prompt, then wait for a reasonable length of time before repeating the prompt or giving a new one.
- The strongest prompting occurs when you use physical assistance or a hand-over-hand technique. This technique is sometimes necessary when someone is first learning a response or action; it is not helpful if used throughout the entire teaching cycle. Try to use this degree of prompting only when necessary and if directed to do so by the family.

Note: Some children do not like to be touched and are upset if someone strongly physically assists them to do something that they do not want to do. If the child already knows how to do something such as untie his shoe, it may be better to give a warning before providing assistance. "Untie your shoe, or I will have to help you. I will count to five. Then I will help you." If the child does not like physical assistance, he may quickly do what has been requested.

The parents can provide guidance regarding prompting to help ensure that your stay with the child is positive and successful.

B. Vicker, *Sharing Information About Your Child with an Autism Spectrum Disorder*, 2007. Shawnee Mission, KS: Autism Asperger Publishing Company, www.asperger.net

Why Are Specific Food Items on the Forbidden List?

Children with ASD can have the same allergies as other children. Allergies are noted with high frequency in the medical histories of many children with ASD. The children might be allergic to environmental allergens, such as pollen, mold, dust, cat hair, and so forth. The most common strategy for dealing with environmental allergens is to avoid them. The same holds true for food allergies. Some children are allergic in varying degrees to soy, wheat, dairy products, or other food substances. Consequently, parents want their child to avoid eating or touching these products.

Sometimes a child is not diagnosed with an allergy but a parent has found a sensitivity to a food or substance that seems to impact the child's behavior, attention, and physical status. Some children are kept off sugar or certain food dyes because of perceived consequences. Sometimes parents may be trying a new intervention to see if it makes a difference for their child. In the latter case, it may be O.K. to give the child a certain food on one visit but not on a subsequent visit. Be sure to check the current listing of acceptable foods rather than depending on memory and past experiences. It is important to know the following:

- What substances are bad for this child and why?
- How sensitive is the child to exposure? (For example, for a child with a strong peanut allergy, even the smell of peanuts on your breath could cause him to immediately break out in hives.)
- How do the parents avoid/limit exposure for the child?
- How do they manage a reaction?
- Are there hidden sources of the problem substance that you might not consider?

B. Vicker, *Sharing Information About Your Child with an Autism Spectrum Disorder*, 2007. Shawnee Mission, KS: Autism Asperger Publishing Company, www.asperger.net

For example, there may be wheat in some play dough formulas. Soy is in many food products but is labeled as lecithin. Considering that children often touch their faces with their hands or put objects in their mouth, it is especially important to be as cautious as possible. Young children are especially prone to grabbing any food in sight because they are unaware of the consequences of these actions.

Other foods that might be on the forbidden list are those that produce a strong negative reaction from the child. Maybe the child does not like wiggly substances such as Jell-O or doesn't like stringy food such as spaghetti. In the latter case, the child is reacting to sensory issues rather than having a physiological reaction to the food.

Becoming familiar with the list of do's and don'ts regarding food is important with all children, but specifically with children with ASD.

B. Vicker, *Sharing Information About Your Child with an Autism Spectrum Disorder*, 2007. Shawnee Mission, KS: Autism Asperger Publishing Company, www.asperger.net

What Is Pica?

Pica is a term that refers to the eating (i.e., swallowing) of non-edible materials. It is more common with very young children and with children with cognitive impairment (i.e., mental retardation). Some children put things in their mouth but do not swallow; others always swallow or do so occasionally.

Objects that are commonly put into the mouth and swallowed include the following (the list is not inclusive):

- Dirt and sand
- Sticks
- Cigarette butts
- Paper cups
- Contents of open cans
- Animal feces
- Dead bugs or worms
- Discarded food
- Chicken bones from ordinary pieces of chicken that are not boneless
- Apple cores
- Jewelry such as earrings, rings
- Colors, markers, erasers
- Play dough
- Tissues, toilet paper, newspaper, book pages

There are three ways of dealing with pica. The first is the most obvious – *constant supervision*. This is the path that must be followed if the child is young or does not understand the difference between items that may be eaten and those that may not. For safety, this is the only course, unless one is 100 percent certain, based on numerous hours of observation of the child, that pica is not a persistent or occasional behavior.

B. Vicker, *Sharing Information About Your Child with an Autism Spectrum Disorder*, 2007. Shawnee Mission, KS: Autism Asperger Publishing Company, www.asperger.net

The second alternative involves *keeping the child in a very sterile or restrictive environment.* This is not completely practical, although it would be easier to achieve in one's home than in the community. Homes like this will have many things locked away in cabinets, and you will need to be careful not to leave anything lying around that was not there when you got to the home.

The last alternative takes time and only works with some individuals. This strategy involves *teaching the child to identify what is food and what is not food.* The child must be able to understand this concept with 100 percent accuracy and remember it when she sees things that she has previously eaten. This strategy is called "cognitive training."

The same alternatives of supervision, restrictive environment, and teaching are options if a child only mouths objects but doesn't swallow. It is better to get the child to not put the off-limits object into his mouth than to try to get him to spit it out without accidentally swallowing it. Sometimes mouthing behavior is more of a bid for attention than a need to experience the taste or shape of the object. Keeping the child occupied and providing him with lots of automatic positive attention may reduce negative attention-seeking behavior. He will feel less of a need to get attention by letting you see that he has put something in his mouth. Otherwise, based on past experience, the child knows it is a fun game to keep someone from getting the object out of his mouth. If mouthing objects is a sensory issue, the parents should have something safe that is available for the child to mouth or chew on. The child should have free access to this object and be redirected back to it if he attempts to put other non-designated items in his mouth.

The parents should be able to provide good advice about this topic area since they will be very concerned about the safety of their child.

B. Vicker, *Sharing Information About Your Child with an Autism Spectrum Disorder,* 2007. Shawnee Mission, KS: Autism Asperger Publishing Company, www.asperger.net

Why Should I Be Concerned About What Jewelry and Clothing I Wear?

P arents are concerned about your safety and well-being as well as that of their child. If a parent advises you to avoid wearing certain types of jewelry and clothing when taking care of their child, take such advice seriously.

In this connection, there are several things to remember about some children with ASD:

- Some children understand very little language, including your request to "stop" what you perceive as a bothersome or hurtful behavior.
- Some children have a difficulty stopping themselves from doing something, even if they have understood your comments or remember their parents' rules. They may have something called a "movement difference" and have difficulty letting go once they have a hold on an object.
- Some children, due to sensory issues, are VERY attracted to certain types of visual stimuli and want to touch the intriguing object and manipulate it in their hands.
- Some children find some objects offensive according to their own personal taste or rules.
- Some children latch onto whatever they can that is handy when they are upset.

The consequence of any of these possibilities includes the following:

- The zipper on your top might be pulled down.
- The child may attempt to pull out your nose stud since it violates her sense of what should be on one's nose.

B. Vicker, *Sharing Information About Your Child with an Autism Spectrum Disorder*, 2007. Shawnee Mission, KS: Autism Asperger Publishing Company, www.asperger.net

- Earrings may be yanked since the dangling objects are colorful and move about when you shake your head.
- The child may attempt to pull the colorful neon slogans off of your T-shirt.
- The child may pull your necklace until you are almost choked.
- The stripes on your shirt may be mesmerizing to the child, and he may have difficulty shifting his attention to other activities.
- If the fabric of your sweater is soft and fuzzy, the child may love to touch it and pull at the fabric nap.

The parents have given you this information sheet for a reason. Be sure to ask what specifically presents a problem.

B. Vicker, *Sharing Information About Your Child with an Autism Spectrum Disorder*, 2007. Shawnee Mission, KS: Autism Asperger Publishing Company, www.asperger.net

Section III
Examples of Information Sharing by Two Families:

Day-of-the-Event and Background Information

- **Adam, Age 6**

- **Jordan, Age 10**

Sample Case – 1
Adam

- **Day-of-the-Event Information**

- **Background Information by Topic**

Day-of-the-Event Information

Date: December 31

- Emergency Information and Contacts

- Permanent Contact List

- Today's Contact List

- The Flow of the Day

- Schedule for Today

- Medications to Be Given

- Possible Activities for Today

- Food for Today

- Behavioral Issues (duplicate set in Background Information section)

Emergency Information

You are at the home of <u>Stephen & Jennifer Mason</u>

Our address is <u>928 Cherry Hill Drive, zip code: 54401-7812</u>

Our phone number is <u>335-7671</u>

Our child's doctor is <u>Dr. Samuel Powers, Phone: 333-0055</u>

Our child's name is <u>Adam Mason Age: 6</u>

For emergencies (fire, police, ambulance), call 911; Adam is #21 on the First Responder's registry. He does not wear a tracking device.

Inform emergency personnel that the child has the following special needs/medical problems:
- Autism
- Seizures
- Asthma
- Low muscle tone; fatigues easily from walking
- Allergy to gluten, yeast, egg and corn - can get aggressive after exposure
- Decreased sensitivity to pain
- Sensitivity to sunlight
- Immune deficiency
- Sensitivity to touch - DO NOT TOUCH HIS HEAD UNLESS NECESSARY; GIVE WARNING, BEFORE TOUCHING
- Sensitivity to loud noises - DO NOT USE LOUD VOICES OR SIRENS, IF POSSIBLE

Height: 45 inches   **Weight:** 44 pounds   **Blood Type:** A Positive

My child takes the following medication/dosages:
- Ventolin inhaler, 2 puffs three times each day, as needed
- Tegretol chewable tablets (100 mg), two tablets twice each day
- Prozac liquid, 1/2 teaspoon (10 mg) each morning
- Melatonin chewable (1 mg), 1 tablet at bedtime

For Poison Control, call 800-758-1212

Permanent Contact List

(See Today's Contact List for where people are located today and whom to call first.)

<u>Name</u>	<u>Relationship to Child</u>	<u>Phone Number</u>
Jennifer Mason	Mother	Cell 332-4498
Stephen Mason	Father	Cell 332-5629 Work 337-1719
Ronald & Fay Mason	Paternal grandparents	Home 336-6059
Thomas & Mary Ann Jennings	Maternal grandparents	Home 333-4173
Bryan & Sheri Wright	Uncle and aunt	Home 336-8778
Donna Spencer	Neighbor	Home 335-1932
Andrea Hawkins	Neighbor	Home 335-2035
Stephanie Abrams	Family friend	Home 336-1583

Today's Contact List

Date: December 31

I/we plan to be home by approximately 1:30 a.m.

I/we will be at the following:

Place	Time	Phone Number
Stephanie Abrams	7-9 p.m.	336-1583
Jefferson Hotel — New Year's Eve Party	9 p.m.-1:30 a.m.	331-3000

Call backup support in the following order. Phone numbers are listed on the Permanent Contact List unless another number is listed here.

First: Mother or father's cell phone

Second: Paternal grandparents

Third: Donna Spencer

Fourth: Andrea Hawkins

The Flow of the Day

Date: December 31

Who will be in the house when you arrive, who will be coming home or leaving and when.

Only Adam will be home. His sister will be at a sleepover at the home of Kirk and Jill Risley. If she needs to be picked up for any reason, tell the parents to call our cell phones.

Any anticipated deliveries, repair workers, etc.

None

Special information peculiar to today that may help you work with/ support my/our child.

We babysat Adam's cousins this morning. The morning was hectic. The boys enjoyed playing with the train display, play-dough, and chasing Adam around the house. Adam may prefer more solitary and quiet play this evening. Refer to the Relaxation page.

Schedule for Today

Date: December 31

Do not change the sequence of the schedule unless it is an emergency or you have completely prepared Adam for the change.

Adam has a copy of the schedule and will expect it to be followed.

Time	Event/Activity
6:30	**Dinner**
7:00	Quiet play time - interactive or solitary
8:00	Bathtime: brush teeth, toilet
	Reward for bath - 10 minutes to look at book on his own - his picture encyclopedia
8:40	Story time in his room - three books; they are on his nightstand; sit on bed while reading
9:00 - ish	End of bedtime routine for Adam

- Get Adam into sleeping bag on top of his bed; zip it 2/3 up; he can show you
- Be sure he has his bear in his arms
- Turn on the air purifier
- Be sure to leave on the little lamp on the dresser
- Turn on relaxation tape (tape player on the dresser)

New since the last visit by a respite worker (i.e., pet, new baby, new skills, new frustrations for child)

- New toys for Christmas. Toys shelves were rearranged but are labeled.
- Adam has had a cold and still has a runny nose.

Medications to Be Given

What Medication	How Much	When	How Given
Ventolin inhaler	2 puffs	7 p.m.	See the diagram taped to mirror in Adam's bathroom
Tegretol chewable	2 tablets	6:30 p.m.	Make sure Adam chews completely with meal before swallowing; count to 10 for him
Melatonin chewable	1 tablet	8:00 p.m.	Before brushing teeth, have Adam chew the tablet for a count of "1-2-3-swallow;" follow with a sip of apple juice

Possible Activities for Today

Date: December 31

Offer a choice for activities marked by an *. Offer combinations of two choices.

Activity	Material Needed	Routine, Adaptation & Location
Checkers*	On 3rd shelf of his bookcase	Let him choose color
Legos*	On 2nd shelf in his room	Adam must disassemble when done
Dominoes*	On 3rd shelf of his bookcase	You go first
Drawing*	Plastic box labeled "drawing" in family room	Remind him to put the covers back on the markers
Paint by number*	Plastic box labeled "painting" in family room	Make sure he matches paint and number
Books*	On shelf in his bedroom	Follow his lead
Puzzle	In family room on 2nd shelf rolled in a green mat	Remind him of need to be careful

Food for the Day

Date: December 31

Food Allergies – DO NOT GIVE ANY QUANTITY OF THE FOLLOWING TO MY CHILD:

Any products that contain wheat. See sticker system. Red stickers on everything with wheat.

OFFER THE FOLLOWING FOODS:

Dinner: Hot dog (no bun) + catsup (offer 2)
Green beans - 1/2 cup
Peaches - 1/2 cup
Banana muffin (made without flour; on counter) - 1
Pickle - 1
8 oz glass of milk - 1
Pudding cup - 1

Rule: Adam must chew 5 times before swallowing, except for liquids.

Remember - Tegretol tablet must taken with food

Snack - None needed since late dinner (see Today's Schedule). If Adam gets up hungry in middle of night, give him up to three cubes of cheddar cheese (refrigerator) and a sip of water.

Free Access All the Time:
- A sip of water when requested, but no more than 4 oz of water after supper.

My Child Eats His Food with the Following Adaptations or Allowances:
- Use his blue cup with Thomas the Tank Engine.

- Use a white plate for food - provides good visual contrast for food item.

Behavior Summary for Adam

Behavior	Purpose	Strategy
Screaming	Protest a demand, request, or situation	Advance visual information, timer, calming area, assistance, Social Story™ (later)
Hitting or other aggressive acts	Protest a demand, request, or situation	Advance visual information, relaxation, calming area, Social Story™ (later)
Pacing	Attempt to relieve anxiety; often related to boredom or lack of knowing how to occupy self	Redirection, structure, choice
Ignoring	If conscious effect - to avoid demand. If very absorbed - may not hear you	Conscious effort - advance warning, timer, visual input; self-absorbed - touch cue and visual information; repeat
Masturbation	Reduce anxiety; sensory	Redirect to his room - privacy
Spitting at you	Same reasons as hitting and screaming	Intervene early, advance visual information, redirection, relaxation, calming area, Social Story™ (later)
Walking into the street	Desire to explore	Close supervision; door locked, visual information

Description of Problem Behaviors

- Screaming – Adam screams for a variety of reasons:
  - When a demand is placed on him that he does not like
  - After being given a food that contains wheat, egg, yeast, or corn
  - When frustrated because something is not as he expects it to be
  - When he is in sensory overload or has experienced an invasion of his personal space
  - When he has to wait
  - When he is touched lightly or on his head
  - When the seams of his clothing bother him

  Note. Sometimes we don't know why he screams.

- Hitting and other aggressive acts – Reasons same as above. He may bump up against someone to get sensory input, however.

- Pacing – Unwilling to follow directive such as to "go play;" needs more specific direction. The more unstructured or chaotic the situation, the more anxiety he will have. He is headed for a meltdown if he begins to flap his arms and make noises.

- Ignoring – Pretends he hasn't heard the directive to do something, especially about taking a bath and getting ready for bed. In some highly stimulating situations, however, such as when he is playing computer games or watching a video, he may not hear our voices.

- Masturbation – Repeatedly rubs his hands over his genital area.

- Spitting at you – Spits at you for the same reasons as the hitting and screaming, but this behavior is likely to occur if ignoring has not been successful. Spitting occurs before he escalates to hitting and screaming. He's not that good at spitting, so it would be rare for spit to land on someone's person unless one is very close.

- Walking into the street – Just walks out the door and plays in the yard; he will go walking in the street if he sees something interesting, or if he thinks you are coming to take him back inside. The outside door is always shut and triple locked. The door will buzz if it is opened. He is told a rule that he must ask permission to go outside and must be accompanied by an adult.

Sample Summary of Behavior Interventions Used with Adam

Visual information – Use pictured materials in the form of schedules, choices, or reminders to aid processing and rule compliance. This is particularly true if the information also shows that something Adam likes will follow something he doesn't like. The visual information also provides a structure for him that he finds difficult to devise for himself.

Restating a request plus – Restate a directive but add the visual information above, set a time limit for the avoidance; use a timer, or do both.

Using a timer – A timer is helpful for indicating when a transition or change to another activity will occur. Also, use a timer to mark when one should begin or end a task or to mark how long to engage in the task.

Environmental adaptation – Depending on the behavior, keep offending foods out of his reach, lock doors, use a stroller for outings, provide fidget toys for waiting, avoid crowds, buy clothing that is comfortable, being flexible on conventions such as flushing the toilet (flush when he is out of the room because of the noise), and so forth.

Removal from situation – Being alone or alone in his room can help Adam recover his composure.

Relaxation techniques – Encourage Adam to do whatever will relax him (hanging upside down, jumping on the trampoline, etc.). Giving him some choice also helps him exercise control over his physical discomfort.

Advance information – Let Adam know ahead of time that he will be in a stressful situation and help him plan how to cope if he gets stressed. Social Stories™ or short scenarios can also help him understand what has happened and how to act differently the next time.

Social Stories™ – Use stories that we have written on a specific problem. We have Social Stories about the hygiene issues of spitting, problem solving, and public versus private behaviors. The stories give Adam information in a positive way. (See Gray & White, 2002, in Reference section.)

Exercise - Getting rid of excess energy can help reduce tension buildup before a negative behavior occurs.

Close supervision – This is an ongoing strategy to prevent behaviors from leading to escalation. This means not to let him out of your sight if outside and he is getting agitated.

Relaxation – Relaxation strategies range from 2-3 minutes of controlled deep breathing to sitting in a slightly darkened room with a blanket wrapped around him. There is a menu on a hook hanging by the kitchen cabinet by the window. He is often able to let you know what he needs.

Calming area – Use the guest bedroom. He can lie on the bed, use the bean bag chair, or sit in the rocking chair. It is devoid of breakable and highly stimulating objects. Leave the overhead light on if he wishes. Leave the door ajar so it is easier to check on him. It is probably a good idea for him to stay for at least 5 minutes if he chose this option or if the other relaxation strategies have not worked. Let him relax until he feels he is calm. Check on him at 5-minute intervals. Sometimes he will fall asleep on the bed. Try to limit the nap to 30 minutes or he won't go to bed on time in the evening. We don't let him nap if it is 4 p.m. or later.

Redirection – Direct Adam from something he should not be doing to something that he may find interesting. For example, direct him to the Activities List for the day if he is uncertain of how to occupy himself or is wanting to go outside. Show him on the schedule if and when he can do the desired activity during your respite stay. He may need to wait until I am home tomorrow during the daytime. (He needs to know he cannot seek permission in the middle of the night, just because a parent is home.)

Assistance – Offer help. He can refuse or accept. He can tell you how he would like you to help.

Structure – Provide some guidelines or boundaries for Adam. His schedule represents structure for him. Following the routine so his life is predictable is helpful. Giving him advance warning about transitions or changes also provides structure.

Order of Strategies for Specific Behaviors

(Only two behaviors are described here.)

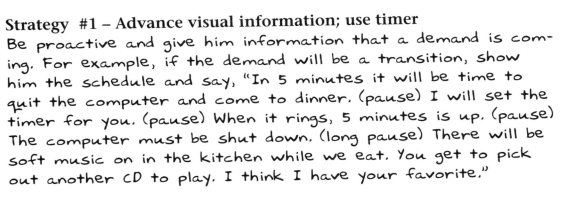

Behavior #1: Screaming when a demand is placed on him *BUT* there is a time for an intervention *before* placing the demand. Situations that fit this scenario include asking Adam to stop playing with the computer.
Generally do Strategy #1 before considering the other options.

Strategy #1 – Advance visual information; use timer

Be proactive and give him information that a demand is coming. For example, if the demand will be a transition, show him the schedule and say, "In 5 minutes it will be time to quit the computer and come to dinner. (pause) I will set the timer for you. (pause) When it rings, 5 minutes is up. (pause) The computer must be shut down. (long pause) There will be soft music on in the kitchen while we eat. You get to pick out another CD to play. I think I have your favorite."

Strategy #2 – Repeat with modification; redirect attention to next activity

If Strategy #1 is not successful and Adam refuses after the 5 minutes, ask if an additional minute might allow him to be at an easy quitting spot in the program. You can only use this strategy if you know the program and good quitting junctures, and don't make it look as though he is controlling the situation. If an easy quitting spot is not available within the next minute or so, request that he save or store the game in memory. He can return to his spot at a later time but maybe not that day. Remind him about what he can do after dinner - use the schedule.

Strategy #3 – Relaxation

Remind him that he can leave the computer. Tell him that you know it is hard because he likes it. It will be easier if he relaxes. Offer him the relaxation menu and encourage him to select one option. Deep breathing might help. If he balks about doing relaxation or the shutdown after it, tell him you will count to 10. Either he shuts down the program or you will. If you shut it down, his place won't be saved and he will have to start all over again tomorrow. It is his choice, but it is time to eat. Offer the relaxation menu again. If he refuses, begin a slow count to 10. Praise him if he responds. If he spits, hits, or screams, go to Strategy #4.

Strategy #4 – Calming area

If Adam is screaming, hitting, or spitting, send him to the guest room to calm down. Return later to shut down and turn off the computer. Check on him in 5 minutes and, if he is calm, let him come to the table for dinner. Have some music playing on the CD player. If he complains about the music, remind him that maybe next time he can choose the music - if he turns the computer off when the timer goes off.

If he is not calm after 5 minutes, give him 5 more minutes. Remind him to find a way to calm himself. Praise him if he has been successful.

Behavior #2: Screaming when a demand is placed on him and there is *no time for advance preparation*.

Adam accidentally knocks over his glass of milk and he is asked to wipe it up with a paper towel. He screams instead. This situation may involve two things – not liking a demand and not liking making a mistake.

Strategy #1 – Relaxation (brief)

Restate the demand in a calm voice and add information as follows: Tell him to get calm and count to 10. (pause) Tell him, "It was an accident, but the milk needs to be cleaned up quickly. The floor and chairs will get sticky and smelly from the milk." Praise him for staying calm and cleaning up the mess. Then give him a replacement glass of milk with the admonition to be careful.

Strategy #2 – Information and assistance

Tell him, "This is no big deal. Let's count to 10 and clean it up together." Praise him if he complies with at least a little of the cleanup. Give him a replacement glass of milk and remind him to be careful.

Strategy #3 – Information and ignoring

Calmly give information and choice, and ignore the screaming. Tell him, "The floor and chairs are sticky. We need to wipe up the milk. Help clean up the mess or no milk with your food tonight." If he doesn't help, be sure you do not give more milk for that meal; give him water.

Strategy #4 – Calming area

If he continues to scream, send him to the guest room to calm down. If he balks, tell him that either he walks on his own or you will help him go. Check on him in 5 minutes. Do not give him milk if he returns to the table. He will have to drink water with his meal. If he screams in protest, send him back to the guest room or ask him to do something else to calm himself.

Later, after things are calm, tell him that accidents happen to everyone: "When one happens, a person needs to clean it up and go on. When you spill something, you have to clean it up or ask someone to help." The family has a Social Story™ that can be used with him about spilling accidents; we will use it later.

(See Gray & White, 2002, in Reference section.)

Background Information – Adam

This section is updated as needed. A copy may be given in advance to the respite worker. A copy is kept in the notebook behind the Day-of-the Event information.

- Family Information
- Family Routines
- Medical and Disability Information
- Self-Help – Eating
- Self-Help – Toileting
- Self-Help – Bathing
- Self-Help – Tooth Brushing
- Self-Help – Sleeping
- Communication and Socialization
- Play Skills
- Sensory Issues and Fascinations
- Relaxation
- Transition
- Behavioral Issues (A duplicate copy appears in the Day-of-the-Event section of the notebook.) *You can change the order of where this section occurs or put it in a separate section of the notebook.*

Topic Area: Family Information

Immediate Family Members:

Adam Mason, 6-year-old with ASD
Intelligent child with significant sensory and ritualistic problems. Leery about strangers who come into his house. Often prefers to be by himself. Has no sense of danger.

Stephen Mason, father
An engineer for a local construction firm. He works long hours but sometimes comes home at odd hours to work in his home office. He is also active in community organizations.

Jennifer Mason, mother
Very involved in the local autism parent organization. Is not employed outside the home. Attends local college on a part-time basis.

Kimberly Mason, 6-year-old twin sister
Plays with many children in the neighborhood. Plays well with Adam most of the time. Can be quite bossy. Is very protective of Adam, especially when strangers are present.

Pets:

Nimbly, the hamster. The cage is in the family room. Nimbly stays in his cage when no parent is home.

Elsa, the cat. Loves to roam outdoors; will scratch on door at night to be let in or out.

Other Relatives in Town:

Grandpa and Grandma Mason; live 5 minutes away. They often take the twins on outings on the weekend.

Grandpa and Grandma Jennings; live on other side of town. Both have some health issues but will try to help if an emergency arises. They are more likely to take one twin at a time on an outing.

Topic Area: Family Routines

Dad – Gets up at 5:30 and leaves for work by 7 a.m. Comes home any time between 2 p.m. and 11 p.m. Likes to take the twins swimming at the YMCA every weekend and on some weekday evenings.

Mom – Gets up at 6 a.m. and goes for a run or works out in the family room. Her class schedule varies by semester. She often has meetings during the daytime or evening. Parents of children with autism often call her to talk about their problems.

Adam – Wakes up promptly by 6 a.m. He plays with his trains or jumps on the trampoline until breakfast is ready. Some days he refuses to eat. He boards the bus with his sister at 8 a.m. He returns from school around 3:30 p.m. and is exhausted. He may take a short nap but is not allowed to sleep longer than 20-30 minutes. After eating a snack, he jumps on his trampoline for a few minutes and plays with toys until dinner at 6 p.m. He plays with his sister or father until his bathtime at 8 p.m. He is asleep by 9 o'clock.

Kimberly – Wakes up at 6:45 a.m., eats breakfast, and quickly gets ready for school. After school she plays with neighborhood children if at least one parent is home. After dinner, she plays with Adam and her dad until her bathtime at 7:30 p.m. Lights out occurs at 8:30 p.m., and she is quickly asleep.

Topic Area: Medical and Disability Information

Adam has the following:

- Autism (see handouts provided by the family on this and other topics).

- Seizures – Takes medication. He rarely has a seizure. See the procedures list added to the first aid book for how to manage a seizure. The book is located on the counter by the sink and the seizure section is marked by a yellow sticky note.

- Asthma – Uses inhaler on a daily basis. May need to use a special inhaler if he begins wheezing. See first aid book for instructions; section marked by blue sticky note.

- Sensitivity to sunlight – Must wear 30 SPF sunscreen even on cloudy day. Preferable to have him wear a hat with a visor if he will be outside for over 30 minutes. (The sunscreen is kept in kitchen cabinet to left of sink.)

- Decreased sensitivity to pain – Can seriously hurt himself and not give an indication of pain or that an accident occurred. Needs constant supervision.

- Allergies to gluten, yeast, egg, and corn. Even a small amount of these substances can cause him to be highly aggressive. Best prevention is to avoid these products (see the section on Self-Help – Eating).

- Anxiety and obsessions about certain things such as rewinding video tapes; he takes medication, and we prevent some opportunities to engage in the obsessions.

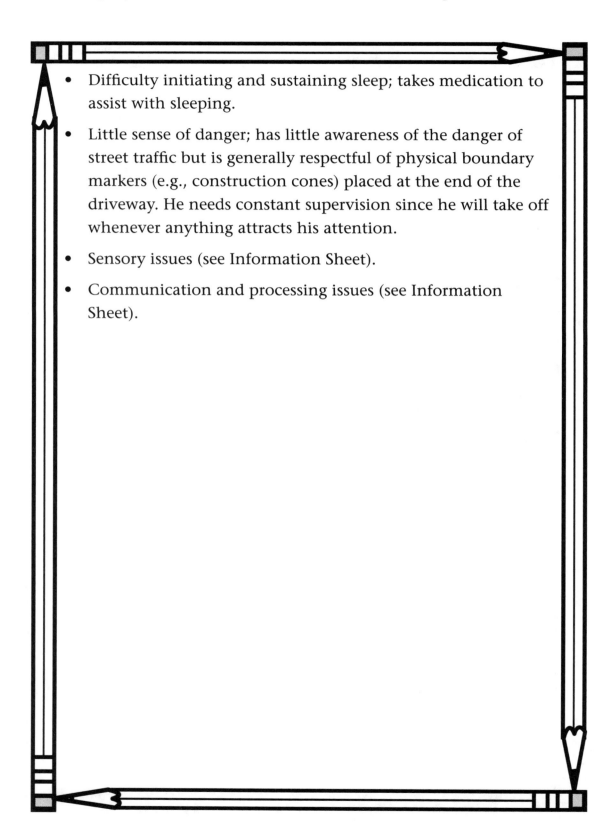

- Difficulty initiating and sustaining sleep; takes medication to assist with sleeping.

- Little sense of danger; has little awareness of the danger of street traffic but is generally respectful of physical boundary markers (e.g., construction cones) placed at the end of the driveway. He needs constant supervision since he will take off whenever anything attracts his attention.

- Sensory issues (see Information Sheet).

- Communication and processing issues (see Information Sheet).

Topic Area: Self-Help – Eating

- Adam is able to eat independently with a fork and a spoon. He is never given a knife for mealtime.

- Adam eats large quantities of food if given the chance. Give him limited portions. Guidelines for proportions are posted on the sheet for the day for food. He does not sense when he is full.

- Adam needs to be supervised because he will stuff his mouth too full. We have taught him some rules to guide the amount per bite or spoonful (see the Food for Today list for current rules).

- Due to his allergies, Adam is unable to eat food that contains gluten (wheat), eggs, yeast, or corn. He has been taught not to eat food labeled with a red sticker for "stop." Nevertheless, be vigilant in case he ignores a sticker or if it has fallen off. Check labels of commercial products for contents to be certain. Any home-baked products must be prepared with substitute products.

- Access to food is limited to specific times of the day: 7:30 a.m., 11:30 a.m., 3:30 p.m., and 6:30 p.m. He is not allowed to wander the house with food, nor is he allowed to graze (i.e., eat a small quantity of food on the run and come back periodically for more). He is to sit at the table for all consumption of food. If he gets up to leave, remove the food and do not give him anything else until the next scheduled meal/snack. His twin sister is held to the same schedule.

- Adam could easily fill himself with water. He is limited to 4-oz juice glass-size portions when he requests a drink. He is limited to two 4-oz glasses between meals, unless he has been outside on a hot day or has been very active.

Topic Area: Self-Help – Toileting

- Adam is able to go to the bathroom on his own and attend to his needs. He does not flush the toilet because he is bothered by the noise. He does not wash his hands in the bathroom. He goes to a container of  Wet Wipes™ and cleans his hands instead of washing. The container is kept in the kitchen on the counter. He may need help pulling one out of the storage container. Please return to the bathroom to flush the toilet for him.

- If out in public, Adam will go into a stall by himself and take care of his needs. Public bathrooms are even more noisy, and he wants to leave as soon as possible. Please quickly flush the toilet and offer a Wet Wipe™ after he is out of the restroom.

Topic Area: Self-Help – Bathing

- You will have to draw the bath for Adam. Only put three inches of warm, room-temperature water into the tub. A few toys are available in the net bag by the tub. The green bag is Adam's.

- Bathtime is limited to 20-30 minutes; set the timer located on the shelf next to the sink. Remind Adam of what the reward is for completing the bathtime routine (see note on Today's Schedule).

- Adam needs help getting into and out of the tub. He is able to wash himself, including giving himself a shampoo. He does not like someone else to touch his head.

- His sister is not allowed to take a bath with Adam.

Topic Area: Self-Help – Tooth Brushing

- Adam is able to brush his teeth on his own. Provide assistance only if he asks for it. He has oral sensory problems, so it is not advisable to manipulate something in his mouth.

Topic Area: Self-Help – Dressing/Undressing

- We buy clothes that Adam can usually manage on his own. Sometimes he needs help with snaps or zippers if he wears something that someone else has purchased for him. Because his shirt may be a little larger than a child his age might typically wear – it is loose rather than tight – he is generally able to independently dress and undress himself.

- He does not take a bath every night. On days when he does not take a bath, he leaves his daytime clothes on to go to bed. This reduces the amount of clothes handling he must do.

Topic Area: Self-Help – Sleeping

- He is given melatonin about 1/2 hour before bedtime to help him sleep. At bedtime, he goes to his room accompanied by an adult and climbs into a sleeping bag on top of his bed. There is a tape recorder on the dresser that plays Christian music. Set the volume to a low level. Leave the table lamp on. Assist him to cover up; only zip the sleeping bag 2/3 closed.

- Leave a light on in every room of the house. If Adam needs to go to the bathroom, he will go on his own. Assist him back to bed if he comes looking for you.

Topic Area: Communication and Socialization

- Adam is able to communicate verbally; often he chooses not to respond. He may not talk much or warm up to a new person until he has met them 3-5 times. It is best to allow him to get to know you in his own way rather than to force interactions or be too overbearing with him.

- Adam processes language at a slower pace and with more difficulty than other children his age. It is best to simplify language when you talk to him. Use short sentences. Use simple vocabulary. Use sign language or pictures to help him understand your message. Repeat the message in different ways, if necessary. Allow time for him to process your message and to respond. Slowly counting to 10 in your thoughts will provide a means of marking wait behavior for you. After a slow mental count of 10, you can repeat the direction.

- Allow Adam to make choices for free-time activities. If he gives you cues that he wishes to play alone, honor that message and let him be. Sit across from him, about 3-5 feet away, and begin to play with something that might be of interest to him (review the Activity sheet for ideas in the Day-of-the-Event section.) It is much better if he chooses to come over rather than try to entice him into an activity that you have chosen. If you know what he likes to do, it will be easier to choose something that might be enticing.

Topic Area: Play Skills

- Adam likes to play with the computer, his GameBoy™ and his toys. He is not allowed to play with any electronics after 7 p.m. because he gets very stimulated from this type of toy. We try to keep him involved in calmer activities after 7 p.m. to facilitate his readiness to go to sleep when put to bed.

- If he wishes to see a video, before 7 p.m., limit the viewing to a maximum of 20 minutes. Do not replay any section of a video for him, even if he asks. Remind him that the rule is, "One time only." This rules helps him from falling into an obsessive pattern of repeatedly viewing favorite scenes. The key to the video cabinet is on a hook in the kitchen inside the cup/glasses cabinet by the sink.

- If he goes outside, remind him to stay inside the yard, which is marked by the yellow soccer/construction cones. Do not leave him unsupervised. He may be outside for no more than one hour.

- If he chooses to swing, be observant for any signs of a seizure such as twitching or jerking of a body part.

Topic Area: Sensory Issues and Fascinations

- It is easy for Adam to experience sensory overload. You will know he's in overload if he begins screaming. It is best to avoid overload. You can do this by being aware of what bothers him, as specified below.

- He is very sensitive to noise. As indicated earlier, he does not want to hear the sound of a flushing toilet. If you see him put his fingers in his ears, it is a clue that something is bothering him. He may also make noises to mask the sound. He does not like any music that includes bass, so be careful of how loud you talk, the volume of the TV or CD player, or sudden loud noises outside, such as a siren, lawn mower, or motorcycle, as these may disturb him.

- Adam is also very sensitive to touch. He likes a firm touch, if one is needed. He gets upset if someone uses a light touch. DO NOT TOUCH HIS HEAD OR HIS CHEEKS without giving him a warning first. He has low muscle tone. As a result, he fatigues easily when walking. In the community, use a stroller as a backup.

- He craves certain types of sensory input, such as bear hugs, jumping on a trampoline, tickles, being bounced (by his dad), and running his fingers over sandpaper letters. (We will provide training to help you know how to best provide this input and when.)

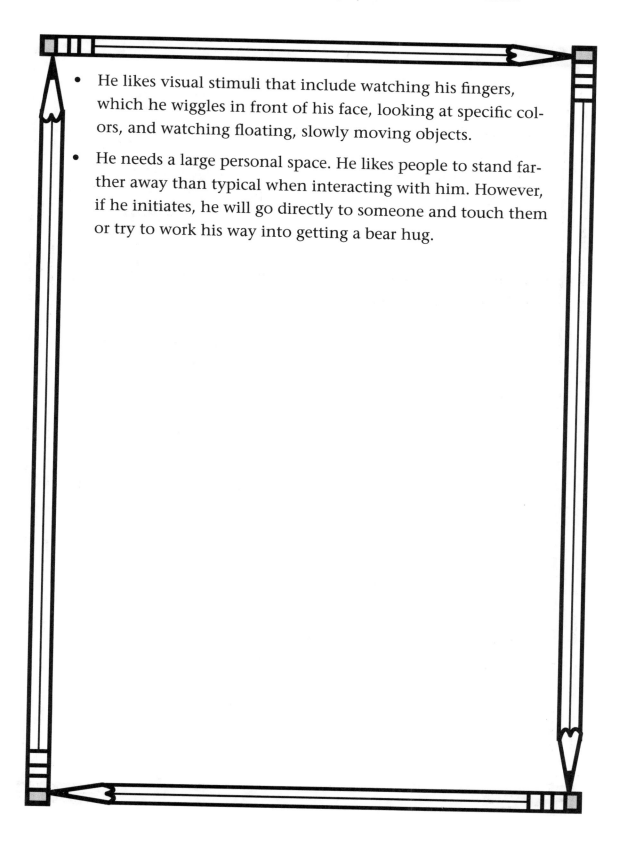

- He likes visual stimuli that include watching his fingers, which he wiggles in front of his face, looking at specific colors, and watching floating, slowly moving objects.

- He needs a large personal space. He likes people to stand farther away than typical when interacting with him. However, if he initiates, he will go directly to someone and touch them or try to work his way into getting a bear hug.

Topic Area: Relaxation

- When Adam becomes overstimulated, it is best to remove him from the situation. When he is at home, he often goes to the guest room and lies on the bed until he feels calm.

- At other times, he prefers to hang upside down on the trapeze bar in the family room, jump on the trampoline, swing, breathe deeply, or get a bear hug. It depends on how upset he is. Ask for his preference, and show him the choice card or menu for relaxation. One is posted inside the respite care notebook; one is located in the family room, the kitchen, and his room on the bulletin board. He may choose one on his own. He is good about giving up the activity when he feels relaxed. When he is upset, he must choose one. If he can't choose, direct him to one of the choices. If he doesn't like it, he will refuse and offer one of the other activities outlined above.

Topic Area: Transition

- Adam is not fond of going places outside of home and school, so getting him into the van to run errands is often a challenge. He is more likely to easily make this type of transition if we are going some place that he enjoys. He also does better at transitioning if he has advance information about the transition site or why he must make a transition.

- He is reluctant to leave activities that mesmerize him, such as the computer. He is aware of how much time he is allowed to play, but he is sometimes great at pretending that he is not aware of the need to transition from this favored activity. It is best to give an advance warning and stick to the time designations on the daily schedule. He has a personal copy of the schedule for the day or the portion scheduled for respite services. Use the schedule to remind him of when he can or will have an opportunity to do the favorite activity again or to complete a game/project. Unfortunately, sometimes that may not be until the next day and this will not be an incentive to stop, so entice him by showing something on the schedule that he enjoys.

Topic: Behavior

We have only included behavior information once – in the Day-of-the-Event section. You can choose to repeat the section in both areas or set up a separate section of the notebook for this topic.

The Behavior sections were constructed using Worksheet A and B1-3.

Sample Case – 2 Jordan

- **Day-of-the-Event Information**

- **Background Information by Topic**

Day-of-the-Event Information

Jordan – July 25

- **Emergency Information and Contacts**

- **Permanent Contact List**

- **Today's Contact List**

- **Flow of the Day**

- **Schedule for Today**

- **Medications to Be Given**

- **Possible Activities for Today**

- **Food for Today**

- **Behavior – Problems, Interventions, Strategies**

Emergency Information and Contacts

You are at the home of <u>Jonathan and Leslie Wilson</u>

Our address is <u>2828 Smith Lane, zip code 64751-2379</u>

Our phone number is <u>848-6697</u>

Our child's doctor is <u>Dr. Terrance Jones Phone: 847-6172</u>

Our child's name is <u>Jordan Wilson Age: 10</u>

For emergencies (fire, police, ambulance), call 911

He is not on any registry, nor does he wear a tracking device

Inform emergency personnel that my child has the following special needs/medical problems:

- Autism
- Environmental allergies - pollen, dust mites, mold
- Food allergy - soy products
- Acid reflux
- Anxiety
- Stomach problems
- Seasonal affective disorder

Height: 56 inches   Weight: 77 pounds   Blood Type: O positive

Our child takes the following medication/dosages:

- Celexa, 1 tablet (10 mg) each morning for anxiety
- Zyrtec, 1 tablet (5 mg) each morning for allergies
- Zantac, 1 tablet (150 mg) twice each day for reflux and stomach problems
- Strattera, 1 capsule (40 mg) each morning for concentration/focus problems

For Poison Control, call 800-716-1212

Permanent Contact List
(See today's Contact List for whom to call first)

<u>Name</u>	<u>Relationship to Child</u>	<u>Phone Number</u>
Leslie Wilson	Mother	Cell 848-3333
Jonathon Wilson	Father	Cell 817-4145 Office 848- 5000
Gladys Shields	Grandmother	847-6607
Amy Fletcher	Neighbor	848-3621
Patty Thompson	Aunt	Cell 817-0055
Mary Showers	Neighbor	848-2189

Today's Contact List

Date: July 25

I plan to be home by approximately 4 p.m.
I will be at the following:

Place	Time	Phone Number
Parent Autism Group Mtg at Borders Bookstore	10:00 a.m. - 12 p.m.	Cell phone: 848-3333 Store phone: 847-3210
Lunch - Chi-Chi's	12:00 - 1:30 p.m.	Use cell phone number
Errands - Corner Stone Mall	1:30 - 3:30 p.m.	Use cell phone number

Call backup support in the following order or depending on the problem. Phone numbers are listed on the permanent contact unless another number is listed here.

First: Call neighbor, Amy Fletcher
Second: Call father at work, Jonathon Wilson

The Flow of the Day

Date: July 25

Who will be in the house when you arrive, who will be coming home or leaving and when.
Sara will be home and she will babysit Timothy.
Timothy may still be sleeping when you arrive.
Sara will take Timothy to the neighbor's at 1 p.m. when she leaves for her swimming lesson.

Any anticipated deliveries, repair workers, etc.
None anticipated.

Special information peculiar to today that may help you work with/support my/our child.
Keep him inside and keep the thermostat at 65 degrees to keep him cool.

If he asks about our vacation, take him to the calendar and count the days until the red-circled date when we go to California.

Anything new since the last visit by a respite worker (e.g., pet, new baby, new skills, new frustrations for child)
Jordan is extra grumpy without the structure of the school day. Be sure to follow the schedule closely to give him comfort.

Schedule for Today

Date: July 25

Do not change the sequence of the schedule unless it is an emergency or you have completely prepared Jordan for the change. Jordan has a personal copy of the schedule and will expect it to be followed.

Supervise at all times.

Time	Event/Activity
10:00	Craft/art activity; then break (free choice)
11:00	Exercising to Richard Simmons tape
11:30	*Computer time; must choose one program and stay with it. Discourage him if he fixates on a single screen
12:00	Lunch for everyone; Sara will help with Timothy
1:00	Looking at books; joint or solitary reading
1:30	Cooking activity; make a dessert for dinner; box mix, ingredients and mixer on counter; hand-wash the dishes from the activity - Jordan can wash and dry items
2:00	*Game - Memory, Connect 4, Candyland, or other choice. When tired of game, put on music and free-style dance for light exercise
3:00	Computer time - must chose one program and stay with it
3:30	Snack
3:45	Unloading the dryer and folding the towels

Medications to Be Given

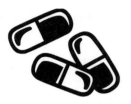

What Medication	How Much	When	How Given

None needed during the scheduled time today. His father will be home for evening administration of meds if I get delayed.

Possible Activities for Today

Date: July 25

Offer a choice for activities marked by an *
on the schedule.
Provide pictured options as demonstrated earlier; see the box on
counter for picture supply.

Computer Games That Are O.K.:
    Crayola 3D Coloring Book
    Dr. Seuss Preschool
    The Pokey Little Puppy
    Muppet Kids - Same and Different

Board/Active Games:
    Connect 4   Operation
    Memory   Cootie
    Candyland   Silly 6 Pins
    Chutes and Ladders   Lotto

Activity	Material Needed	Routine & Adaptation & Location
Board Games	In family room - on shelf with Jordan's name sticker	Remind him of how to play; remind him that he may win or lose but it is fun to play together.
Computer	In family room	Turn on, log in as "Jordan."

Food for Today

Date: July 25

Food Allergies – DO NOT GIVE ANY QUANTITY TO MY CHILD OF THE FOLLOWING:

Nothing with soy products - no margarine, peanut butter, or commercially baked materials

OFFER THE FOLLOWING FOODS:

Lunch

Chicken noodle soup
(soup on counter; heat in microwave)
Banana (on counter)
Carrot sticks (in crisper)
Carrot bread (no soy in it) (1-3 slices) (on counter)
12-oz glass of milk

Snack: Cheese squares - limit of 10 (in refrigerator
on 3rd shelf)
Apple slices (cut up) - apples in dish on counter;
knife in right-hand drawer by sink (put dirty knife in
bag labeled "dangerous, dirty tools" in refrigerator; do
not put it in the sink)
8-oz glass of milk

Free Access All the Time:
Upon request, give ice water or ice tea as requested, up to
12 oz in morning or afternoon. Do not let Jordan help himself.

Behavior Concerns – Summary

Behavior	Purpose	Strategy
Screaming loudly	Protest when he can't have his way, when asked to do something he doesn't want to do, being too hot, or too noisy	Prevention: ignoring, schedule, redirection, information, relaxation; time out as last resort
Stripping	Protest being too hot	Prevention: monitor clothing, thermostat control; remove layers as needed
Shattering objects & dropping eggs	Sensory	Keep all breakable objects out of sight; redirect
Wandering	Boredom	Redirect; engage
Replaying favorite video scenes over and over	Pleasure from repetition - obsessive behavior	Rule about no repetitions or TV goes off; tapes locked away
Hitting	Protests various things	Depends on what he is protesting; use timer, redirect
Shredding paper	Attention seeking	Provide attention proactively; keep paper inaccessible
Destroying property	Arousal - relief from boredom, opportunity, curiosity	Intervene when restlessness begins; redirect to more active activity

Description of Problem Behaviors

- **Screaming** – Jordan screams when he is in sensory overload or when he is bothered by certain types of stimuli. He has very good hearing and is annoyed when the TV, music, conversations, or environmental noise is too loud for him. It may not seem too loud to a person with average hearing ability. There is a series of cues in Jordan's behavior before screaming occurs: He usually makes comments about something being too loud; he growls if the noise continues, and begins to scream if the noise does not subside. He refuses to wear ear plugs. He is difficult to take to many events/settings in the community.

- **Stripping when hot** – Jordan will strip off all his clothes if he is excessively hot from the weather, exercise, and indoor/outdoor conditions. He seems to feel most comfortable with a room temperature of around 65 degrees, which is usually too cool for other family members. He is irritable in the summer with high humidity and high temperatures.

- **Stripping when wet** – Jordan does not like his shirt to be wet. If it is wet from water, a juice spill, or perspiration, he will strip off the shirt, and if anything is on his pants, they will come off too. Clothes are supposed to have a certain feel, and only certain clothes will do. Everything hanging in his closet or in his drawers is O.K. clothing for him to wear without objections.

- **Shattering glass objects** – Jordan likes to break glass objects to see the visual pattern and to hear the crashing sound. He is more likely to do this when he feels he wants attention. He needs constant supervision. Most objects that could be broken have been put away, but occasionally someone might forget.

- **Dropping eggs** – Generally, we do not keep any eggs in the house. Jordan loves to smash eggs on the floor and is excited by the color contrast and splash pattern of the eggs on the floor.

- **Wandering** – Jordan likes to go outside, particularly if it is cool. It is not safe for him to be out unsupervised. He will wander off to a store if he thinks there is something that he wants. He will wander into traffic without checking for danger. He would probably wander off with a stranger. We have a door chime on the door so you can hear if someone exits. Also, the door to the outside is always locked and he does not breach it.

- **Replaying favorite scenes** – If given free access, Jordan will rewind a video to his favorite part numerous times in a row. He is not allowed free access to the tapes, DVDs, or computer programs.

- **Hitting** – Jordan is more likely to hit his younger brother in order to gain access to a specific toy. He is likely to hit others when he is tired, overstimulated, or very determined to get his way. He generally hits with an open hand rather than a clenched fist. He generally swipes someone rather than hitting them with a closed fist.

- **Shredding paper** – Although one might have predicted that Jordan would throw small pieces of shredded paper like confetti, this is not what happens. Instead, he likes to shove a small piece of paper into his ear. This may be more for attention than for sensation because he will make sure someone is looking when he does it. Unless it is easy to pluck the piece of paper out, he will need to have the paper removed by his doctor.

- **Destruction of property** – If unsupervised, Jordan likes to explore drawers, cabinets, storage boxes, and closets. He will open bottles of shampoo, throw stuff on the floor, scatter or smear substances, and so forth. Some doors are always locked. He needs constant supervision.

Summary of Behavior Interventions Used with Jordan

Ignoring – Do not give eye contact or look directly at Jordan. Pretend you haven't noticed what he is doing.

Redirection – Direct or assist Jordan to move onto another activity or go to another location. The objective is to get his attention diverted from what we don't want him to do and redirected toward something more acceptable. Sometimes redirections are just reminders of what he needs to be doing. In other cases, the redirection is a distraction and has to be interesting enough to compete with what is currently the focus of his attention. For example, if he is starting to shred paper, suggest that you put on a music video and dance. For the moment, leave the shredded paper on the floor; clean up with or without his help later.

Visual support – Provide a visual display that helps him process a message or information and/or guides his behavior. This might be a schedule, choice board, chart, picture, text, gesture or sign language.

Timeout – Remove Jordan to the red chair in the living room, kitchen, or family room (three identical chairs to make life easier). Set the timer for 10 minutes. Do not give him any attention during the 10 minutes. If he is calm, he is directed to whatever is appropriate. Provide a reminder of the rule. For example, the rule is, "No jumping on the sofa; jump on the trampoline."

Relaxation – Remove Jordan from the overstimulating situation. Allow him to choose between the following options: He can sit in his bean bag chair and listen to music with earphones until he is more relaxed OR he can choose to be alone to relax in his room.

Schedule information – When Jordan needs to know if and when an event will happen or end, refer to the schedule. Write a note to me on the wipe-off board in the kitchen if it is not an event for the day of respite service schedule.

Timer – Use a timer when Jordan needs to stay with a task for a certain amount of time or when something MUST terminate in a specific amount of time. A good example is a time limit for being outside.

Explanation – Provide information in a concise, direct manner. For example, "It's cold outside. You must wear your blue jacket."

Routine consequences – If Jordan does something wrong, the object involved is removed from the situation. For example, if he keeps bouncing the ball near the china cabinet despite redirections, remove the ball. A different consequence is that if he makes a mess, he must clean it up. For example, if he throws popcorn around the family room, the TV goes off, and he has to pick up the popcorn before the TV is turned back on.

Rule – Remind him of a specific rule such as no repetition of video scenes. (He has worn out videos with this obsessive behavior.)

Preventive measures – Keep things locked up, absent, or otherwise inaccessible. Also note behavior, and if there is a suggestion that agitation or excitement is growing, redirect to another activity or relaxation, or interact with him if it is a bid for attention.

Adaptation – Use a Walkman, deep pressure with a blanket or sheet, or other sensory activities to help cope with over- or excessive stimulation.

The best behavioral intervention is to adjust the environment to prevent the behavior from occurring.

Order of Strategies for Specific Behaviors for Jordan

Not all behaviors will be discussed in this sample case study. Some behaviors are controlled by preventive measures; others occur infrequently. For demonstration purposes, only the high-frequency situations are discussed.

Behavior #1: Screaming when the environment is noisy

Strategy #1 – If the noise cannot be stopped immediately, use redirection and/or relaxation

Jordan can be redirected to another area that is more quiet. If he needs to calm down/relax, he can choose between the following options: He can sit in his bean bag chair and listen to music with earphones until he is more relaxed OR he can choose to be alone to relax in his room.

Strategy #2 – Schedule information and timer

If he has not yet followed the direction to leave the area, let him know that the noise will persist for X amount of time. He can wait it out until there is a change of activity or go do something else until it is quiet. You can set the timer for how long the noise will last (provide for a margin of error by adding a few extra minutes).

Strategy #3 – Information, adaptation, and relaxation

If he cannot avoid being in the noisy situation, he will need to do something to mask the noise. Provide explanations about the noise. He can go get his Walkman and listen to music to mask the noise. Suggest that he do something to relax while listening to the music. This might be wrapping himself with a sheet, sitting in a rocking chair, or asking for a backrub.

Behavior #2: **Stripping when hot & screaming**

Be sure the respite worker knows:
- Where the thermostat is located and how to adjust it.
- The location of any fans, if they are safe to use when Jordan is around.
- What your definition of "stripping" is.

Prevention
- Be sure Jordan is dressed in layers.
- Watch for cues that he is getting overheated. If he appears to be flushed and restless, suggest he remove a layer.
- Adjust the thermostat and let him know that you are doing that.

Strategy #1 – Information
Provide information in a concise, direct manner. For example, "You can take off your T-shirt but not your shorts. It will be cooler soon."

Strategy #2 – Redirection
Direct or assist Jordan to move on to another activity or go to another location after removing a layer or two and adjusting the thermostat. The objective is to get his attention diverted from thinking about being hot to doing something he likes.

Background Information – Jordan

This section is updated as needed. A copy may be given in advance to the respite worker. A copy is kept in the notebook behind the Day-of-the-Event information.

- Family Information

- Family Routines

- Medical and Disability Information

- Self-Help – Eating

- Self-Help – Toileting

- Self-Help – Bathing

- Self-Help – Tooth Brushing

- Self-Help – Sleeping

- Communication and Socialization

- Play Skills

- Sensory Issues and Fascinations

- Relaxation

- Transition

- Problem behaviors (duplicate of what appears in Day-of-the-Event section)

Topic Area: Family Information
(see page of photos in Jordan's miniature photo album)

Immediate Family Members:
Jordan Wilson, 10-year-old with ASD. Called "Jordie." Generally happy unless his routine is upset, then he's anxious and can be belligerent and aggressive. Currently likes the Care Bear characters.

Jonathon Wilson, father
Often out of town. Works as auditor for an accounting company.

Leslie Wilson, mother
Works part time for the same accounting firm as her husband but from her home office.

Sara Wilson, 12-year-old sister
Attends middle school; active in sports. Can be a big help with Jordie. Is often not home because of various practices and lessons.

Timothy Wilson, 3-year-old brother
Has high interest in Thomas the Tank Engine. Attends a local preschool. Is gentle with Jordie but often gets into fights when Jordie grabs one of his train cars or other toys.

Pets:
Sebastion, the dog, indoor, friendly Lab; called "Bassie" by Jordie.

Chelsey, the cat, indoor, reclusive tabby, called "C.C." by Jordie.

Other Relatives in Town:
Uncle Bob and Aunt Patty; live nearby. Their children are the twins **Matt** and **Charlie**, age 5. Jordan sees them often. They have a dog named **Jacque.**

Grandpa and **Grandma Wilson;** live about 20 miles away. Grandpa collects miniature trains and Grandma plays lots of bridge. They are very active in the community and often travel out of town in their RV.

Topic Area: Typical Family Routines

Dad – If in town, leaves at 7:30 a.m. and returns home around 6 p.m. Often has evening meetings as he serves on several community boards. Likes to watch sports and news on TV to relax.

Mom – Gets up around 6 a.m. to make breakfast and get the children off to school. Does her office work in the morning while the oldest two are at school and Timmy is at a preschool. Afternoons are spent with errands, housework, and meetings with Timmy in tow. She may attend Sara's games in the afternoon or evening, if she has respite care. She is also active in the local chapter of the Autism Society of America (ASA).

Jordie – Gets up at 6 a.m. every day. He watches a video until breakfast is ready. He gets dressed and puts out food and water for the pets. He anxiously waits for the school bus, which arrives around 7:25 a.m. He returns home by 3:30 p.m. and immediately wants a snack. He relaxes in his room for about 30 minutes. He plays quietly or lies on the bed. When he has recovered from the stress of the school day, he goes outside and walks around in the backyard. If Mom is home, he does homework or draws while Mom is preparing dinner. After dinner, he may play with his Care Bear miniature figures, jump on the trampoline, or help his parents with a few chores before bathtime. He takes a bath at 8 p.m., which is followed by stories read to him in his bedroom.

One story must always be his favorite Care Bear book; he chooses one other picture/story book and his mom or dad chooses one. Lights are usually out by 9 p.m.

Sara – Leaves the house on a school day by 7 a.m. Some days she is home by 3:30 p.m., but many days it is 6 p.m. or later. On weekends, she likes to sleep until 10 a.m. if she doesn't have a game. She studies with a neighborhood girlfriend some days.

Timmy – Gets up at 7 a.m. and attends preschool from 9:00-12:00. He takes a nap most afternoons. He attempts to play with Jordie in the evening. He is able to occupy himself with Legos, books, and imaginative play. He goes to bed at 8 p.m. after his bath and story time.

General House Rules

- No jumping on the sofa.

- No friends in at night when parents are away.

- No viewing violent or adult-oriented TV programs in the family room, even when Jordan is in bed because he is apt to get up and return to the family room for reassurance or guidance to the bathroom.

Topic Area: Medical and Disability Information

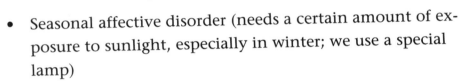

Jordan has an autism spectrum disorder. In addition, he has difficulty with:

- Anxiety (takes medication – Celexa)

- Allergies (takes medication – Zyrtec)

- Acid reflux (takes medication – Zantac)

- Frequent stomach problems (takes medication – Zantac)

- Seasonal affective disorder (needs a certain amount of exposure to sunlight, especially in winter; we use a special lamp)

- Cognition – learns more slowly than someone of his age level; understands at a level more like a child in kindergarten; has poor problem-solving skills

Anxiety

- Jordan shows that he is anxious by pacing back and forth more, flapping his hands, and talking to himself. The more intense the anxiety, the more irritated and potentially explosive he becomes. Violation of routines and the schedule are prime sources for increases in anxiety. He is learning to tell people what is bothering him, but only does so if an adult asks him leading questions.

Allergies

- Jordan is allergic to pollen, dust mites, mold, and soy products. An air purifier runs at all times in his room and in the family room. During times of high pollen count, his outside time is restricted.

- Symptoms of his allergies include low energy, sneezing, rubbing his eyes, and/or significant headaches.

Acid Reflux

- Acid reflux is more likely to happen when Jordie is asleep. He may wake up crying with an awful taste in his mouth. If so, take him to the bathroom to rinse out his mouth; he may or may not be willing to drink some water.

Stomach Problems

- Certain foods upset Jordie's stomach. Forbidden items are listed on the Food for Today list.

Topic Area: Self-Help – Eating

- Jordie is independent in eating, and uses a fork and spoon as needed.

- He tends to eat quickly and needs to be reminded to slow down.

Topic Area: Self-Help – Toileting

- Jordan is somewhat independent in toileting. He goes on his own but needs help with wiping himself after a bowel movement.

- He tends to go to the bathroom once every hour or so because he drinks a lot of liquids when he is home.

Topic Area: Self-Help – Bathing

- Although Jordie can turn on faucets, it is preferable that you run his bathwater for him; otherwise he tends to make the water too hot and the tub too full. About half a tub with a capful of bubble bath is fine.

- Jordie can wash himself in the tub. We do not shampoo his hair in the tub but by the sink.

- Jordie takes a shower only if there is no alternative, or if he must be cleaned up quickly.

- He likes to play with his toys in the tub. Bathtime in the tub needs to be limited to 1/2 hour.

Topic Area: Self-Help – Tooth Brushing

- Jordie is able to get his own tooth-brush ready and brush his teeth.

- He needs some supervision to prevent him from repetitively refilling his toothbrush and watching the paste and spit run out of his mouth into the sink.

Topic Area: Self-Help – Dressing/Undressing

- Jordie is able to undress himself independently; he needs assistance with untying his shoes and unbuttoning some jeans.

- Jordie is usually independent in dressing but may need help with some zippers or pants buttons. He needs someone to lay out a couple of shirts to go with a pair of pants; then he can make a choice. This helps give him some control.

Topic Area: Self-Help – Sleeping

- We read stories in his bedroom from 8:30 until 8:55 p.m. He is ready for lights-out and goes right to sleep by 9 p.m.

- Jordie does not always stay asleep, however. If he wakes up, he wants to go downstairs to play. HE CANNOT BE LEFT DOWNSTAIRS WITHOUT SUPERVISION. He must either stay with an adult downstairs, or an adult must go back to his bedroom and stay with him until he falls back to sleep.

Topic Area: Communication and Socialization

- Jordan usually uses speech for communication. He primarily uses 2- to 4-word sentences but may also use some longer memorized phrases. When not understood, he can be asked to (a) repeat his message, (b) show you what he wants, and (c) get his communication book. The latter functions as a backup system. The book is kept in the bottom left-hand drawer of the cabinet next to the sink in the kitchen. Since he doesn't use the book very often, he may not remember where it is located. He may need reminders of the meaning of the picture cues.

- Jordan is reasonably social. He prefers to be where the family is. If you invite him, he may watch an activity from a few feet away for 5-10 minutes before being willing to join an activity. With his younger brother, he is more likely to be attracted to his toys and approach more quickly to grab something. His younger brother usually lets him grab things but often protests. Jordan is still learning about taking turns and sharing. He used to prefer to be alone or twirl things; now he only does this when he is uncomfortable or anxious. Every time you visit, it may take a few minutes for him to warm up.

Topic Area: Play Skills

- Although Jordan still has some interest in Thomas the Tank Engine toys and books, he prefers to spend time on the computer. We limit the amount of time he can use the computer. He also likes to watch videos or DVDs. (Check the list of what is available for the day and any scheduled viewing; this list is posted on the TV set so you don't need to return to the kitchen to locate the information.) Videos are kept in a locked cabinet in the living room; you will be given the key upon arrival. Jordan is not allowed access because he likes to rewind tapes and repeatedly replay favorite sections. He also likes building with Legos and manipulating miniature figures. He is attracted to the Care Bears because of the designs on their stomachs. He also likes to repeat their names such as Cheer Bear, Tender-Heart Bear, and so forth.

- He plays some matching/simple board games if they are not too complicated or do not take too long (too long is defined as 15-20 minutes on good days). He likes it if someone reads to him. Choose books that are more suited for someone about 5-6 years old. He also reads easy books by himself and listens to favorite children's songs on CDs. (The easy books and CDs are in his room; the shelves are clearly marked.)

Topic Area: Sensory Issues and Fascinations

- Jordan likes visual sensory stimulation. He particularly likes to see splash and breakage patterns. He loves to smash eggs on the floor and break things such as glass figurines. We often encourage him to paint and look at a kaleidoscope to provide acceptable substitute sensory activities.

- He likes to shred small pieces of paper and stuff them into small places such as his ear, vents, and so on.

- He is sensitive to indoor and outdoor temperatures and strips if he is too hot; he is oblivious to social convention.

- If his shirt is wet, he wants it removed immediately.

Topic Area: Relaxation

- Jordan likes to sit in a bean bag chair to relax. He can be cued to do some deep breathing exercises on his own. Going for a walk or lying on his bed is also relaxing to him.

Topic: Transition

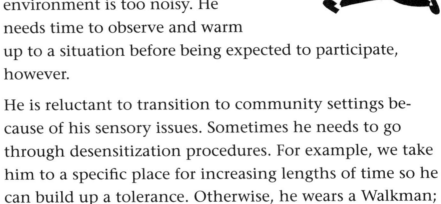

- As long as his picture schedule is used, Jordan usually does not have major problems with transitions around the house. He likes to be with people, even in new situations, except when, according to his standards, the environment is too noisy. He needs time to observe and warm up to a situation before being expected to participate, however.

- He is reluctant to transition to community settings because of his sensory issues. Sometimes he needs to go through desensitization procedures. For example, we take him to a specific place for increasing lengths of time so he can build up a tolerance. Otherwise, he wears a Walkman; if he gets his birthday wish, he will use an iPod™. He uses music to mask uncomfortable noise.

- The exception to the easy transitioning occurs when he is very locked into a sensory sensation. He will be very reluctant to abandon that activity. We try to proactively give him the stimulation that he needs through activities that are acceptable to the family. The shredding can be very mesmerizing, so we may redirect him to the kaleidoscope or the trampoline.

Topic Area: Problem Behaviors

This material was prepared using Worksheets A and B1-3. A copy of Jordan's material is located in the Day-of-the-Event section. To avoid duplication within this book, it is not reproduced again in this section for readers.

In real-life situations, it would be wise to put this same information in both sections of the notebook for respite workers and to consider putting it in a prominent location within each section. Another alternative is to produce one copy and put into a separate tabbed section entitled Behavior Management.

Section IV

Blank Forms

Emergency Information and Contacts

You are at the home of _____

Our address is _____

Our phone number is _____

My child's name is _____ Age: _____

My child's doctor is _____ Phone: _____

For emergencies (fire, police, ambulance, lost child), call 911.

_____   Let them know my child has a tracking system (please describe how system is used)

_____   Let them know my child is on the local autism first responders' emergency registry (please describe)

Emergency personnel will want to know that my child has the following special needs/medical problems:

Height: Weight: Blood Type:

My child takes the following medication/dosages:

For Poison Control, call _____

B. Vicker, *Sharing Information About Your Child with an Autism Spectrum Disorder*, 2007. Shawnee Mission, KS: Autism Asperger Publishing Company, www.asperger.net

Permanent Contact List

(See today's Contact List for where people are located to-day and whom to call first)

Name   **Relationship to Child**   **Phone Number**

B. Vicker, *Sharing Information About Your Child with an Autism Spectrum Disorder*, 2007. Shawnee Mission, KS: Autism Asperger Publishing Company, www.asperger.net

Today's Contact List

Date:

I /we plan to be home by approximately _____.
I /we will be at the following:

Place   **Time**   **Phone Number**

Call backup support in the following order or dependent on the problem; the latter will be explained to you. Phone numbers are listed on the emergency list unless a new number is listed here.

First:

Second:

Third:

Fourth:

B. Vicker, *Sharing Information About Your Child with an Autism Spectrum Disorder*, 2007. Shawnee Mission, KS: Autism Asperger Publishing Company, www.asperger.net

The Flow of the Day

Date:

Who will be in the house when you arrive, who will be coming home or leaving and when.

Any anticipated deliveries, repair workers, etc.

Special information peculiar to today that may help you work with/ support my/our child.

Anything new since the last visit by a respite worker (i.e. pet, new baby, new skills, new frustrations for child).

B. Vicker, *Sharing Information About Your Child with an Autism Spectrum Disorder*, 2007. Shawnee Mission, KS: Autism Asperger Publishing Company, www.asperger.net

Schedule for Today

Date:

Do not change the sequence of the schedule unless it is an emergency or you have completely prepared my child for this change.

_____   My child has a personal copy of the schedule and will expect it to be followed.

<u>Time</u>   <u>Event/Activity</u>

B. Vicker, *Sharing Information About Your Child with an Autism Spectrum Disorder*, 2007. Shawnee Mission, KS: Autism Asperger Publishing Company, www.asperger.net

Medications to Be Given

What Medication	How Much	When	How Given

B. Vicker, *Sharing Information About Your Child with an Autism Spectrum Disorder*, 2007. Shawnee Mission, KS: Autism Asperger Publishing Company, www.asperger.net

Possible Activities for Today

Date:

Offer a choice for activities marked by an *.
Provide pictured options as demonstrated earlier.

Activity	Material Needed & Where Located	Routine or Special Adaptation

B. Vicker, *Sharing Information About Your Child with an Autism Spectrum Disorder*, 2007. Shawnee
Mission, KS: Autism Asperger Publishing Company, www.asperger.net

Food for Today

Date:

Food Allergies – DO NOT GIVE ANY QUANTITY TO MY CHILD OF THE FOLLOWING:

OFFER THE FOLLOWING FOODS:
(Provide a pictured choice for the following foods – a box of food pictures is located _____)

Breakfast

Lunch

B. Vicker, *Sharing Information About Your Child with an Autism Spectrum Disorder*, 2007. Shawnee Mission, KS: Autism Asperger Publishing Company, www.asperger.net

Food for Today (continued)

Dinner

Snack

Free Access All the Time:

My child eats his food with the following adaptations or allowances:

Topic Area: Family Information

(See examples in Sections I and III)

B. Vicker, *Sharing Information About Your Child with an Autism Spectrum Disorder*, 2007. Shawnee Mission, KS: Autism Asperger Publishing Company, www.asperger.net

Topic Area: Family Routines

(See examples in Sections I and III)

B. Vicker, *Sharing Information About Your Child with an Autism Spectrum Disorder*, 2007. Shawnee Mission, KS: Autism Asperger Publishing Company, www.asperger.net

General House Rules

(See examples in Sections I and III)

Topic Area: Medical and Disability Information

(See examples in Sections I and III)

Topic Area: Self-Help and Eating

(For this and subsequent topic areas, see examples in Sections I and III)

B. Vicker, *Sharing Information About Your Child with an Autism Spectrum Disorder*, 2007. Shawnee Mission, KS: Autism Asperger Publishing Company, www.asperger.net

Topic Area: Self-Help and Toileting

B. Vicker, *Sharing Information About Your Child with an Autism Spectrum Disorder*, 2007. Shawnee Mission, KS: Autism Asperger Publishing Company, www.asperger.net

Topic Area: Self-Help and Bathing

Topic Area: Self-Help and Tooth Brushing

B. Vicker, *Sharing Information About Your Child with an Autism Spectrum Disorder*, 2007. Shawnee Mission, KS: Autism Asperger Publishing Company, www.asperger.net

Topic Area: Self-Help and Dressing/Undressing

B. Vicker, *Sharing Information About Your Child with an Autism Spectrum Disorder*, 2007. Shawnee Mission, KS: Autism Asperger Publishing Company, www.asperger.net

Topic Area: Self-Help and Sleeping

Topic Area: Communication and Socialization

Topic Area: Play Skills

B. Vicker, *Sharing Information About Your Child with an Autism Spectrum Disorder*, 2007. Shawnee Mission, KS: Autism Asperger Publishing Company, www.asperger.net

Topic Area: Sensory Issues and Fascinations

B. Vicker, *Sharing Information About Your Child with an Autism Spectrum Disorder*, 2007. Shawnee Mission, KS: Autism Asperger Publishing Company, www.asperger.net

Topic Area: Relaxation

Topic: Transition

B. Vicker, *Sharing Information About Your Child with an Autism Spectrum Disorder*, 2007. Shawnee Mission, KS: Autism Asperger Publishing Company, www.asperger.net

Worksheet A: Behavior Concerns – A Summary

Behavior	Purpose	Strategy/Intervention

B. Vicker, *Sharing Information About Your Child with an Autism Spectrum Disorder*, 2007. Shawnee Mission, KS: Autism Asperger Publishing Company, www.asperger.net

Worksheet B-1: Description of Problem Behaviors

B. Vicker, *Sharing Information About Your Child with an Autism Spectrum Disorder*, 2007. Shawnee Mission, KS: Autism Asperger Publishing Company, www.asperger.net

Worksheet B-2: Summary of Behavior Interventions

Worksheet B-3: Order of Strategies Used for Specific Behavior

B. Vicker, *Sharing Information About Your Child with an Autism Spectrum Disorder*, 2007. Shawnee Mission, KS: Autism Asperger Publishing Company, www.asperger.net

Section V

Reference Materials

Resource Check-Off List

Most of the following materials should be included in your caregiver notebook. Some material will be specific to particular medical conditions and only included on an as-needed basis. This includes information about managing seizures, extracting foreign substances from your child's mouth, asthma attacks, and so on.

Check with your doctor's office, local hospital, the public health department or some other reliable source to obtain materials for the notebook. Required material will be dependent upon the needs of your child. Check the date of any printed material to be sure it's up-to-date and that your child's doctor agrees with the recommendations.

Typical Information to Include

Check if it applies to your child and family situation; mark X if you have completed this section or gathered this information.

☐ Contact information for yourself, backup people, first responders' emergency registry (if applicable) or tracking agency (if applicable)

☐ Your child's schedule

☐ Food guidelines

☐ Activity suggestions

☐ Current first aid book; should be located next to the notebook

☐   Specific management of your child during an asthma attack (if applicable)

☐   Specific management of an allergic reaction to food or environmental substances, if applicable

☐   Specific management of your child to remove foreign substances from mouth

☐   Specific management for choking

☐   Specific management of a seizure

☐   Behavior management strategies for specific situations

☐   Updated emergency phone numbers

☐   Specific information on sensory issues, bedtime routines, etc.

First Aid/Emergency Procedures Resources

- It is advisable to have a current book available as a reference guide that describes the latest techniques for first aid/emergency intervention. Single-page charts are often inadequate to provide enough current information, and it is not practical to go online to one of the reliable websites when in the middle of an emergency. Although respite workers should have training in first aid, it is advisable to have a visual support reference handy so the person does not need to depend on memory, especially as his anxiety increases.

Three books to consider include:

  - Krohmer, J. R. (Ed.). (2004). *American College of Emergency Physicians first aid manual* (2nd American ed.). New York: Dorling Kindersley.

  - Krohmer, J. R. (Ed.). (2003). *American College of Emergency Physicians pocket first aid*. New York: Dorling Kindersley.

  - John Hopkins Children's Center. (2002). *John Hopkins Children's Center first aid for children fast* (rev. ed.). New York: Dorling Kindersley.

- Ask the respite worker for proof of current first aid/CPR certification card.

- Be sure emergency phone numbers and important information are placed in a prominent location by the phone.

- Discard first aid books and charts published prior to 2000.

References for Respite Personnel

Below are a few classic references and websites for the individual respite worker who wishes to read some introductory information. Books and websites are constantly being developed so you may wish to add new favorites that you think are helpful as you find the material.

Books on Autism Spectrum Disorders

Attwood, T. (2007). *The complete guide to Asperger Syndrome.* London: Jessica Kingsley Publishers.

Barron, J., & Barron, S. (1992). *There's a boy in here.* New York: Simon & Schuster. (Written by a mother and son with ASD)

Biel, L., & Peske, N. (2005). *Raising a sensory smart child.* New York: Penguin Books.

Elliott, L. B. (2002). *Embarrassed often, ashamed never: Quick and short stories from one family's ongoing adventure with Asperger Syndrome and autism.* Shawnee Mission, KS: Autism Asperger Publishing Company.

Grandin, T. (1995). *Thinking in pictures and other reports of my life with autism.* New York: Doubleday. (Written by an adult with autism)

Sakai, K. (2005). *Finding our way: Practical solutions for creating a supportive home and community for the Asperger Syndrome family.* Shawnee Mission, KS: Autism Asperger Publishing Company.

Shore, S. (2003). *Beyond the wall: Personal experience with autism and Asperger Syndrome* (rev. ed.). Shawnee Mission, KS: Autism Asperger Publishing Company. (Written by an adult with autism)

Sicile-Kira, C. (2004). *Autism spectrum disorders.* New York: Berkley Publishing Group.

Wing, L. (2001). *The autism spectrum: A parent's guide to understanding and helping your child.* Berkeley, CA: Ulysses Press.

Reliable Websites for General Information about Autism Spectrum Disorders

Autism Society of America: http://www.autism-society.org

Center for the Study of Autism: http://www.autism.org

Division TEACCH: http://www.teacch.com

Indiana Resource Center for Autism: http://www.iidc.indiana.edu/irca

National Institute of Mental Health: http://www.nimh.nih.gov/healthin-formation/autismmenu.cfm

Recommended Reading

The author used her experience as an autism consultant and parent to write much of this book. At the same time, the results of many years of reading, attending conferences, and other types of professional exchange have been incorporated. The following, in particular, may give parents additional ideas about how to communicate with respite workers to ensure the best possible care of their child with ASD.

Baker, B. L., & Brightman, A. J. (2004). *Steps to independence: Teaching everyday skills to children with special needs* (4th ed.). Baltimore: Paul Brookes Publishing Company.

Ernsperger, L., & Stegen-Hanson, T. (2004). *Just take a bite: Easy, effective answers to food aversions and eating challenges.* Arlington, TX: Future Horizons, Inc.

Gray, C., & White, A. L. (2002). *My social stories book.* Philadelphia: Jessica Kingsley Publishers.

Lieberman, L. A. (2005). *A "stranger" among us: Hiring in-home support for a child with autism spectrum disorders or other neurological differences.* Shawnee Mission, KS: Autism Asperger Publishing Company.

Myles, B. S., Cook, K. T., Miller, N. E., Rinner, L., & Robbins, L. A. (2000). *Asperger Syndrome and sensory issues: Practical solutions for making sense of the world.* Shawnee Mission, KS: Autism Asperger Publishing Company.

Myles, B. S., & Southwick, J. (2005). *Asperger Syndrome and difficult moments: Practical solutions for tantrums, rage, and meltdowns* (rev. ed.). Shawnee Mission, KS: Autism Asperger Publishing Company.

Myles, B. S., Trautman, M. L., & Schelvan, R. L. (2004). *The hidden curriculum: Practical solutions for understanding unstated rules in social situations.* Shawnee Mission, KS: Autism Asperger Publishing Company.

Rouse, C., & Katera, P. (1997). *Quick and easy: Ideas and materials to help the non-verbal child "talk" at home.* Solana Beach, CA: Mayer-Johnson Company.

Seligman, M., & Darling, R. D. (1989). *Ordinary families, special children: A systems approach to childhood disability.* New York: The Guilford Press.

Smith, C. (2003). *Writing and developing social stories: Practical interventions in autism.* Oxon, UK: Speechmark Publishing, Ltd.

Wheeler, M. (1998). *Toilet training for individuals with autism and related disorders: A guide for parents and teachers.* Arlington, TX: Future Horizons, Inc.

Finally, a Handbook for Hiring One-to-One Support for Children and Young Adults with Disabilities

A "Stranger" Among Us

Lisa Ackerson Lieberman, MSW-LCSW

Hiring one-to-one providers to support your child is not work for the faint of heart, but finding the right person is worth every bit of effort involved. And *A "Stranger" Among Us* shows you how. Based on years of personal experience, research, and interviews with parents and providers, Lisa Lieberman has written a one-of-a-kind book that demystifies what could otherwise be an overwhelming task – finding the best one-to-one support for a child or young adult with disabilities.

A "Stranger" Among Us will show you how to:

- Decide what kind of support your child needs
- Develop a job description that aligns with your family's values and needs
- Get the word out about the job opening
- Screen for quality candidates
- Conduct a productive interview
- Check references
- Set up in-home communication and train providers

Using examples, checklists, and sample questions, Lieberman creates a framework from which a family can assess its needs and core values before moving forward with the recruitment, hiring, training, supervision, and retention of quality one-to-one support and respite care that best fits its needs. Obtaining care for loved ones is a critical process, and "Stranger" covers a complex topic with sensitivity and understanding.

Lisa Lieberman, MSW, LCSW, is a trainer, writer and speaker with over twenty-nine years of experience. Along with a private counseling practice in Oregon, Lisa travels nationally to present on issues related to living with disability in the family. She has been married since 1979 to a man with multiple sclerosis. Together they parent Jordan, a wonderful eighteen-year old son with autism.

Autism Asperger Publishing Company
877-277-8254 (toll-free) • www.asperger.net

AAPC Exclusive

The best-selling practical solutions series continues to offer sound, practical advice for and about individuals with ASD and other social-cognitive disorders. These titles offer a range of topics – from sensory issues to social situations and education to behavior –

Asperger Syndrome and Difficult Moments: Practical Solutions for Tantrums, Rage, and Meltdowns (Revised and Expanded Edition)

Brenda Smith Myles and Jack Southwick

Code 9901B   Price: $21.95
Code 9720 (DVD)   Price: $29.95

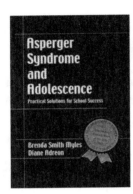

Asperger Syndrome and Adolescence: Practical Solutions for School Success

Brenda Smith Myles, Ph.D., and Diane Adreon

Code 9908   Price: $23.95

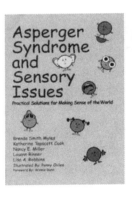

Asperger Syndrome and Sensory Issues: Practical Solutions for Making Sense of the World

Brenda Smith Myles, Katherine Tapscott Cook, Nancy E. Miller, Louann Rinner, and Lisa A. Robbins

Code 9907A   Price: $21.95

Asperger Syndrome and the Elementary School Experience: Practical Solutions for Academic & Social Difficulties

Susan Thompson Moore

Code 9911   Price: $23.95

Autism Asperger Publishing Company

Practical Solutions Series

that address the needs of individuals on the spectrum. These books truly offer "practical solutions" to everyday challenges people with ASD face.

Practical Solutions to Everyday Challenges for Children with Asperger Syndrome

Haley Morgan Myles

Code 9917　　　　　　**Price: $13.95**

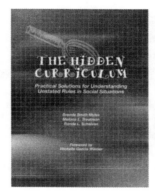

The Hidden Curriculum: Practical Solutions for Understanding Unstated Rules in Social Situations

Brenda Smith Myles, Melissa L. Trautman, and Ronda L. Schelvan

Code 9942 (book)　　　**Price: $19.95**
Code 9721 (DVD)　　　**Price: $29.95**
Code 9968 (calendar)　　see website for price

Perfect Targets: Asperger Syndrome and Bullying; Practical Solutions for Surviving the Social World

Rebekah Heinrichs

Code 9918　　　　　　**Price: $21.95**

Finding Our Way: Practical Solutions for Creating a Supportive Home and Community for the Asperger Syndrome Family

Kristi Sakai

Code 9948　　　　　　**Price: $21.95**

Visit www.asperger.net or call 877.277.8254 to place an order.

APC

Autism Asperger Publishing Co.
P.O. Box 23173
Shawnee Mission, Kansas 66283-0173
www.asperger.net